THE KINGFISHER

YOUNG DISCOVERERS ENCYCLOPEDIA

OF FACTS AND EXPERIMENTS

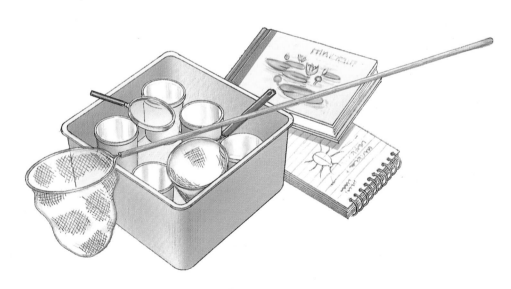

KING*f*ISHER

NEW YORK

KINGFISHER
Larousse Kingfisher Chambers Inc.
95 Madison Avenue
New York, New York 10016

First published in 2000
The material in this edition was previously published
in eight individual volumes in 1993 and 1995.

2 4 6 8 10 9 7 5 3 1

1TR/1299/WKT/—(UNV)/115JMA

Copyright © Kingfisher Publications Plc

LIBRARY OF CONGRESS CATALOGING-IN-PUBLICATION DATA
has been applied for

ISBN 0-7534-5301-0

Printed in Hong Kong

Contents

ENERGY AND POWER 7

BATTERIES, BULBS, AND WIRES 33

SOUND AND LIGHT 59

RIVERS AND OCEANS 131

SOLIDS AND LIQUIDS 85

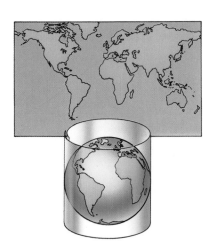

About This Book

This book looks at the world of science in everyday life. It suggests lots of experiments and things to look out for in order to help you discover more about natural processes and natural resources.

You should be able to find nearly everything you need for the experiments in and around your home. Be sure to ask an adult to help you when we suggest doing so—some of the experiments could be dangerous to do on your own.

Activity Hints
- Before you begin an experiment, read through the instructions carefully and collect all the things you need.
- When you have finished, put everything away and wash your hands.
- Start a special notebook so that you can keep a record of what you do in each experiment and the things you find out.

ENERGY AND POWER

What is Energy?

Energy is everywhere. We can see it as light, hear it as sound, and feel it as heat. There are other forms of energy as well, such as electrical, chemical, and movement energy. We use electrical energy for power in our homes and chemical energy, in the form of fuel, to power our cars. But, as you will see, when we use energy, we often do harm to our environment as well.

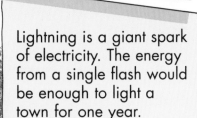

Lightning is a giant spark of electricity. The energy from a single flash would be enough to light a town for one year.

factory

bicycles

tanker

house

We use electrical energy to heat and light factories, offices, schools, and homes. Electricity is also used to light up our streets at night.

Do it yourself

See how energy can be used to make things turn. You must ask an adult to help you when you light the candle.

1. Draw a snake, like the one shown here, on a piece of paper. Cut it out and add a red tongue and two eyes. Then tie a length of thread onto the snake's head.

2. Hang your snake above a lighted candle, keeping its tail away from the flame. Now watch it turn. (Be sure to blow out the candle when you have finished.)

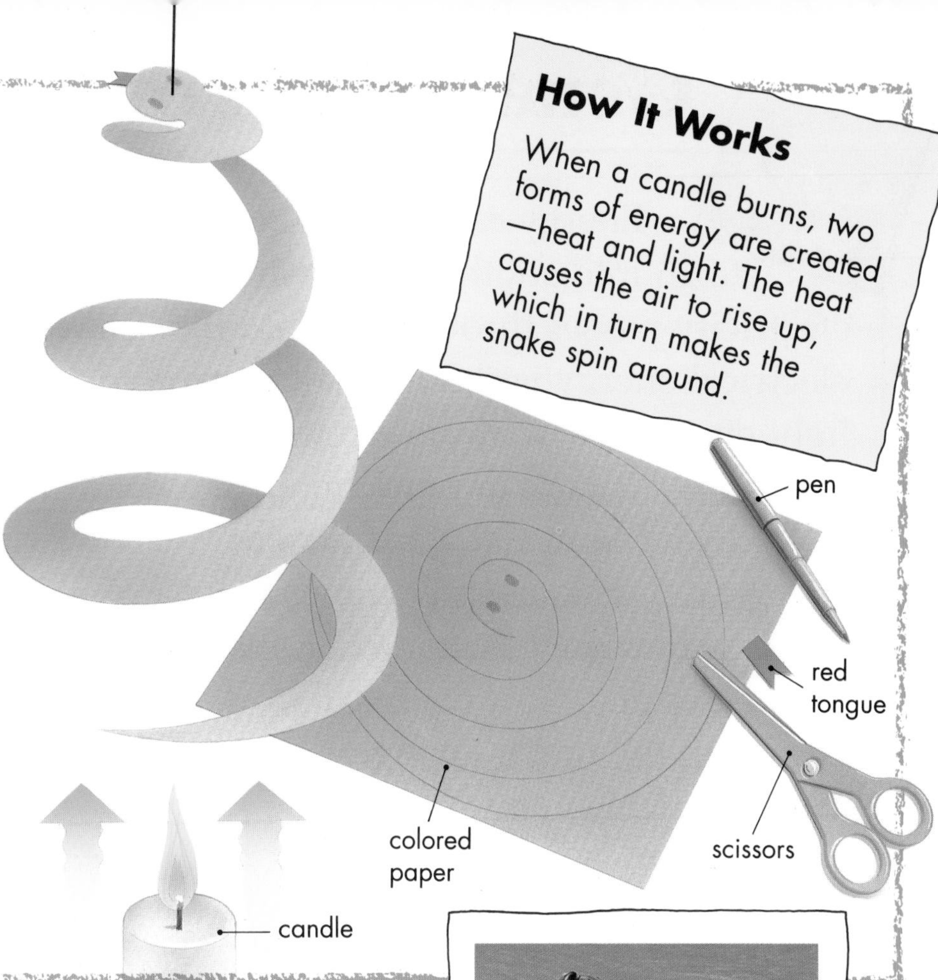

How It Works

When a candle burns, two forms of energy are created —heat and light. The heat causes the air to rise up, which in turn makes the snake spin around.

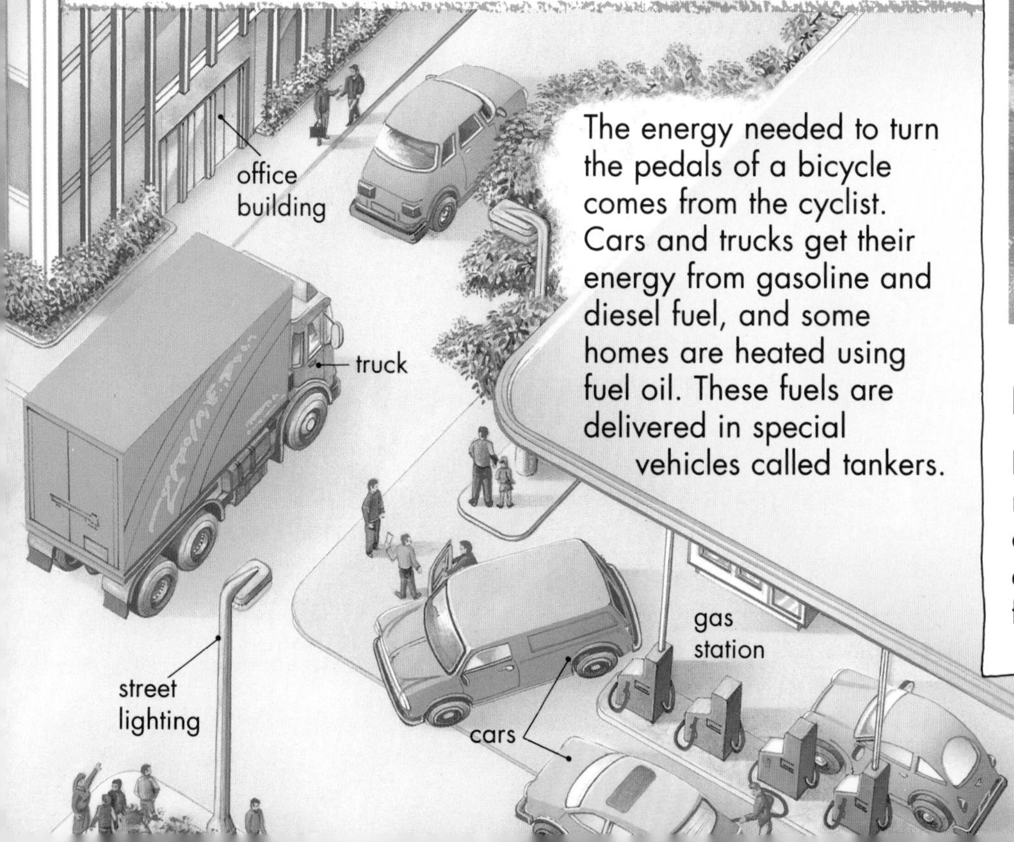

pen

red tongue

colored paper

scissors

candle

office building

truck

street lighting

cars

gas station

The energy needed to turn the pedals of a bicycle comes from the cyclist. Cars and trucks get their energy from gasoline and diesel fuel, and some homes are heated using fuel oil. These fuels are delivered in special vehicles called tankers.

Food for Energy

People use energy to move, keep warm, grow, and stay healthy. The energy we need comes from the food we eat.

Generating Power

Energy can be changed from one form into another. For example, when electricity passes through a light bulb, electrical energy is changed into heat and light energy. Most of the electricity we use today is made in power plants. But power plants need a source of energy, too. This usually comes from fuels such as oil, gas, and coal. Inside the power plant, the chemical energy in the fuel is changed into electrical energy.

cooling tower cools steam

boiler

steam

cables carry electricity

tower

coal supply

steam spins turbine

generator makes electricity

👁 Eye-Spy

Use the energy in your muscles to light up a bulb by fitting a generator light set to your bike. When you ride your bike, the wheels turn and the generator makes electricity.

At a power plant, coal is burned inside a boiler. The heat turns water into steam, which is used to spin a special wheel called a turbine. This in turn drives a machine called a generator, which changes the movement energy into electrical energy. Power lines carry the electricity to homes and factories.

Do it yourself

Make your own steam turbine. You'll need an adult to help you.

1. Cut a circle 3 inches across from a thick foil food tray. Pierce a small hole in the center, then snip in toward the hole with your scissors as shown. Twist the sections slightly to make the blades.

2. Ask an adult to punch two small holes in the top of a full, soda can—one in the center, the other about half an inch to one side. Empty the soda out and pour half a cup of water into the can.

Many power plants have cooling towers. The hot steam cools inside the towers and turns back into water. The water is then pumped back to the boiler where it is heated all over again.

3. To make the stand, cut a piece of thick foil 8 in. long and $1\frac{1}{2}$ in. wide. Fold in half lengthwise, then bend into shape as shown so it fits across the top of the can. Make a small hole 2 in. up on each side of the stand.

4. Fix the stand onto the can with a small screw. Then push a 4-inch-long wooden skewer through the holes in the sides of the stand, threading the wheel in place as you go.

5. Make sure the blades of the wheel are positioned over the small hole in the can. Then ask an adult to put your turbine on a stove burner over a low heat. As the water starts to boil, the escaping steam will spin the wheel on your turbine.

soda can

screw

wooden skewer

stand

blades of wheel

heat

The Price of Power

When fuels are burned to give energy, they release harmful gases that pollute (poison) our air. Often these gases lie above cities, creating a layer of smog (dirty air). Some of the gases mix with water in the air to form acids. When it rains, the acid in the rain damages forests and lakes. Burning fuel also releases the gas carbon dioxide. This is called a "greenhouse gas" because it traps the Sun's heat in the atmosphere (the air around the Earth), just like glass traps heat in a greenhouse. The trapped heat makes the atmosphere warm up, which may cause changes in our weather.

Many children suffer from an illness called asthma. They find it hard to breathe and have to use an inhaler. Doctors think that air pollution may be causing the asthma.

Then and Now

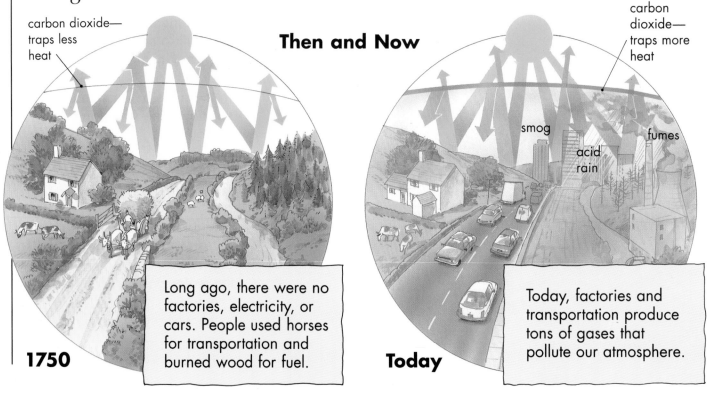

carbon dioxide—traps less heat

carbon dioxide—traps more heat

smog

acid rain

fumes

1750

Long ago, there were no factories, electricity, or cars. People used horses for transportation and burned wood for fuel.

Today

Today, factories and transportation produce tons of gases that pollute our atmosphere.

12

Do it yourself

Try making smog in a glass jar. You'll need to ask an adult to light the paper for you.

1. Find a large jar and wash it out with water. Don't dry the jar though—you want it to be slightly damp.

ice

twist of paper

foil

damp jar

A thick layer of smog hangs over New York City making it difficult to see the buildings clearly.

smog

2. Cut a piece of aluminum foil slightly larger than the top of your jar. Put some ice cubes onto the foil.

3. Cut a small piece of newspaper. Fold it a couple of times then twist it up.

4. Ask an adult to light the paper and drop it in the jar. Quickly seal the jar with the foil and ice and watch what happens. (Don't worry if the flame goes out.)

How It Works

The smoke from the burning paper rises up in the warm air. When it reaches the cold air around the ice, it sinks back down to the middle where it mixes with the water in the air to form smog. When the weather is damp and warm, the same thing happens over cities that produce a lot of smoke and pollution.

13

Nature's Fuels

All living things depend on the Sun for energy. Plants use light energy to make their own food—a form of chemical energy. Animals eat plants so they can use the chemical energy stored inside. The fuels we all depend on—coal, gas, and oil—also contain a store of chemical energy. They are called "fossil" fuels because their energy comes from organisms (plants and animals) that lived millions of years ago. When the organisms died their bodies became buried and their remains slowly turned into coal, gas, and oil.

Oil Underground

Oil is the fossil remains of tiny animals that died millions of years ago. Oil rigs drill down below the ground or seabed and remove the oil.

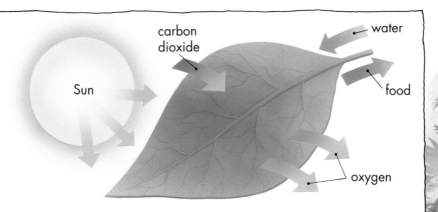

carbon dioxide

water

Sun

food

oxygen

Energy from the Sun

Plants capture light energy from the Sun and use it to make food in a process called photosynthesis. Inside the leaves, the gas carbon dioxide is combined with water to make sugars and a substance called starch. The gas oxygen is produced and released back into the air.

Do it yourself

Do this simple experiment to see whether or not plants need light to grow.

1. Put some damp cotton balls on three glass jar lids and sprinkle a few alfalfa sprout seeds on top.

2. Put one lid on a sunny windowsill, another in a dark cupboard. Cut a small hole in a cardboard box and put the third lid inside. Close up the box.

3. Leave the seeds to grow for a week, keeping the cotton wool damp with a little water.

How It Works

The seeds on the window-sill grow well because they have enough light. Those in the cupboard shrivel and die because, without light, they cannot make food and grow. The seeds in the box grow toward the hole to get as much light as possible.

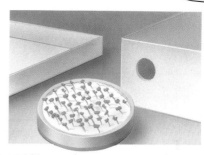

Coal is the remains of plants that lived in swamps millions of years ago. As the plants died, they sunk layer upon layer beneath the water. The weight of the top layers squashed the bottom layer which eventually became much harder, forming coal.

coal seam

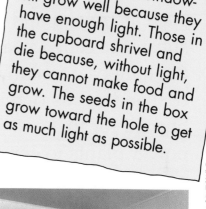

 **Eye-Spy**

Next time you eat bread, cereal, potatoes, pasta, or rice, think about where the food has come from. All these foods contain starch made by plants from the Sun's energy.

Other Natural Fuels

Coal, oil, and gas are not the only fuels that nature gives us. In some parts of the world, such as Ireland and Siberia, people still use a substance called peat. Peat is the first stage in the long coal-making process. It is softer than coal and not as rich in energy, but it can be burned for fuel and is sometimes used in power plants to generate electricity. Wood also makes a good fuel—many people still use it to heat their homes and for cooking.

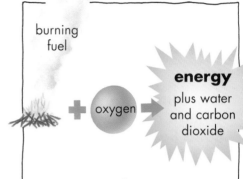

burning fuel

+ oxygen →

energy plus water and carbon dioxide

How Fuels Burn

As we have seen, fuels contain a store of chemical energy. When fuels burn, they react with oxygen in the air and release heat and light energy, plus water and carbon dioxide. The proper word to describe something burning in air is combustion.

Wood is an important fuel in poor countries, where it is collected and burned on fires and stoves for cooking food and boiling water.

Digging for Fuel

Peat is still an important fuel in Ireland, where it is dug up from the ground as small bricklike pieces. The peat bricks are then dried before being burned on fires and stoves in the home.

Low on Fuels

oil

gas

coal

Unfortunately, there is only a limited amount of fossil fuels in the world. Once the supplies have run out they cannot be replaced. This is why fossil fuels are called nonrenewable fuels. Wood is also being used up too quickly. Trees can be replanted but they still take over 50 years to grow. So we need to find alternative sources of energy if we are not to run out of power.

How Much Is Left?

There may be enough coal to last for another 300 years. But oil and gas may run out within the next 50 years.

Do it yourself

Make some paper logs to burn as fuel.

1. Tear some newspaper into strips and put them in a large bowl of hot water. Mash the paper into a pulp with a wooden spoon.

2. Scoop up the pulp using a sieve. Pick up a handful of pulp and squeeze out all the water, forming a log shape as you do so.

3. Make several more logs, then leave them to dry out. Then ask an adult to help you make a fire with them.

How Can We Help?

If we all use less energy then the supply of fossil fuels will last longer. Try to turn off unwanted lights, use the car less often, and wear an extra sweater instead of turning the heat up.

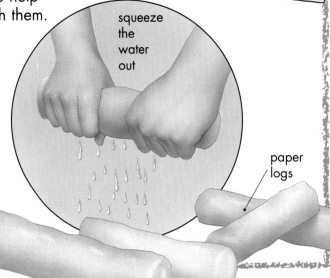

newspaper strips

squeeze the water out

paper logs

17

Splitting Atoms

Instead of using fossil fuels to make electricity, we can use "nuclear power." The energy for nuclear power comes from a metal called uranium. Like all matter, uranium is made up of tiny particles called atoms. When a uranium atom is split into smaller particles, a vast amount of heat energy is released. This can be used to generate electricity. But waste products from nuclear power plants are very dangerous and are difficult to get rid of safely.

Radioactive Waste

Nuclear power produces a dangerous form of energy called radioactivity. This can contaminate (infect) people and animals, making them very sick. Radioactive waste from power plants is marked with this warning symbol.

Energy from Atoms

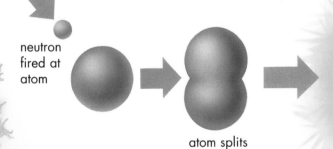

neutron fired at atom

atom splits

heat energy produced

neutrons released

Sun's surface

In a nuclear reaction, tiny particles called neutrons are fired at uranium atoms at very high speeds. They split the uranium atoms, causing them to release more neutrons and lots of heat energy. The neutrons bump into more uranium atoms, causing them to split. This is called a fission reaction. Another type of nuclear reaction, called nuclear fusion, is taking place inside the Sun all the time.

If there has been a leak at a nuclear power plant, scientists use a machine called a Geiger counter to test for radioactivity in the ground and in animals. Sometimes farmers paint their sheep yellow to show they have been contaminated with radioactivity.

The reactor core in a nuclear power plant is surrounded by water. The water is heated by the nuclear reaction.

Making Electricity

In a nuclear power plant, the uranium is placed in rods inside a "reactor core." It is carefully shielded so that the radioactivity cannot escape. The heat from the nuclear reaction heats the water surrounding the core. This hot water is then used to turn water in the heat exchanger into steam. The steam is used to spin the turbines, and electricity is generated.

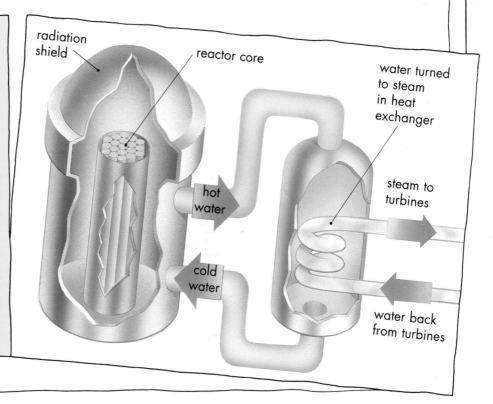

radiation shield

reactor core

water turned to steam in heat exchanger

hot water

steam to turbines

cold water

water back from turbines

Energy from the Sun

The Sun is like a huge power plant, releasing vast amounts of heat and light energy. It supplies a free source of energy that will not run out. Scientists have devised many new ways of making use of solar energy. Solar panels absorb heat from the Sun and heat water for homes and factories. Other panels, called photovoltaics, can change light directly into electricity. Both of these ways of using solar energy produce very little pollution.

👁 Eye-Spy

On a hot sunny day, a garden hose acts like a solar panel. It absorbs the Sun's energy and the water inside heats up. Look out for a cat lying on a hose, enjoying the heat.

Do it yourself

Make some tea using energy from the Sun.

1. Take two clear glass bottles the same size. Paint one of them black. Put two tea bags in each bottle and fill them up with cold water.

2. Put the bottles on a sunny windowsill for at least six hours. If you have a thermometer, test the temperature of the water every two hours to see which bottle heats up quickest. Watch the water turn brown as your tea brews.

tea bags

water

thermometer

How It Works

The Sun's energy heats the water and brews the tea. Because the black glass absorbs heat better than the clear glass, the water in the black bottle will heat up faster and the tea will brew more quickly.

Trapping the Sun's Energy

Simple solar panels, like the one in the diagram, are placed on the roof of a house and used to heat water. The water absorbs heat as it circulates through the pipes in the panel and becomes much hotter.

On a much larger scale, this solar power plant in California does the same thing. Thousands of mirrors reflect the sunlight onto tubes containing a special oil. The oil is heated to 1067°F (575°C) and is used to make steam which, in turn, spins a turbine to make electricity.

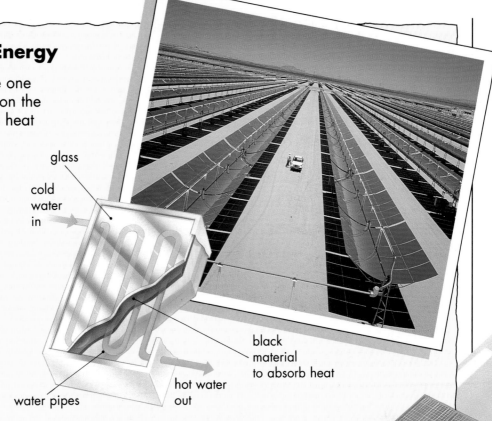

glass

cold water in

water pipes

hot water out

black material to absorb heat

Called the Sunraycer, this strange-looking car is powered by solar energy. It won the first international solar-powered car race in 1987, traveling more than 1,950 miles (3,140km) across Australia.

👁 Eye-Spy

Look out for small items powered by solar energy, such as calculators, watches, and radios. They use photovoltaic cells to convert the light energy into electricity.

Wind Power

The wind is another free source of energy that can be trapped and used to make electricity. People have made use of wind power for hundreds of years. Windmills were once built to turn a large millstone that was used to grind wheat into flour. Small wind-powered pumps are still used to pump water from wells. About 25 years ago, the first modern wind generators appeared in the United States. Since then, many more have been built all around the world. Because the wind will never stop blowing, wind power is an important source of renewable energy.

Windmills

Traditional windmills for grinding wheat are still found in countries such as the Netherlands. This windmill has four large sails to catch the wind.

Wind Farms

A collection of wind generators is called a wind farm. This one is in California, on the mountains behind the city of Los Angeles. It is very windy here, so the area is ideal for wind power.

On a wind farm, each generator has two or three long narrow blades. As the blades turn in the wind, they turn a turbine which generates electricity.

Do it yourself

Make this wind-powered winch and see how you can use the power of the wind to lift objects into the air.

1. Tape a thread spool on its side to the top of a length of wood about 10 inches long.

2. Cut four pieces of cardboard—2 inches x 1 inch, for your blades. Tape each blade onto the end of a toothpick as shown. Then stick the other end of the toothpicks into a cork and twist the blades so that they face each other.

3. Stick the cork onto the sharp end of a pencil. Thread the pencil through the thread spool on the wooden stand. Make sure the pencil turns freely in the hole.

4. Jam a slightly smaller thread spool (complete with thread) onto the blunt end of the pencil. If the hole is too big, wind tape around the end of the pencil to give a tight fit.

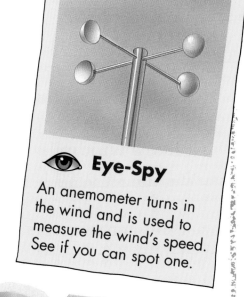

👁 Eye-Spy

An anemometer turns in the wind and is used to measure the wind's speed. See if you can spot one.

materials

5. Unravel about 8 inches of thread from the smaller spool and tie a blob of modeling clay on the end to act as a weight.

6. Blow on the blades to see if your winch can lift the weight. You may need to alter the direction of the blades or make the weight slightly smaller to get your machine to work properly. Now try your machine outside in the wind.

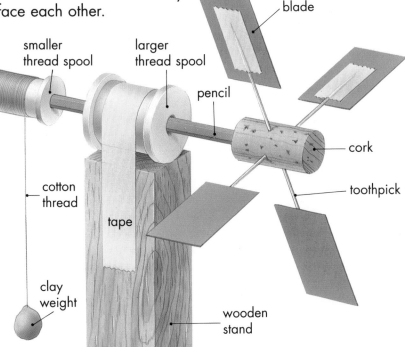

smaller thread spool

larger thread spool

pencil

blade

cotton thread

tape

clay weight

cork

toothpick

wooden stand

The Power of Water

Moving water is an important source of free energy. Hundreds of years ago people built watermills by rivers and used them to grind wheat into flour, just like a windmill. Today, moving water can be used to generate electricity. Huge dams, called hydroelectric dams, are built across rivers to generate electricity for nearby cities. The waters of the ocean are also moving, and waves and tides are now being used as a source of energy.

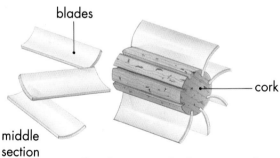

Hydroelectric dams are built across rivers where there is a steep fall in height. The water falling from the top of the dam turns a huge turbine to make electricity.

Do it yourself

Try making your own waterwheel out of a plastic drink bottle. You may need to ask an adult to help you if you find some of the cutting too difficult.

1. Cut a plastic soda bottle into three pieces as shown. The middle section should be 3 inches deep. Now cut four strips, 1 inch wide, out of the middle piece. Cut each strip in half to make eight blades.

plastic soda bottle

middle section

base section

blades

cork

2. Draw eight lines evenly spaced down the side of a cork. Cut slits down the lines with a blunt knife and push a blade into each slit.

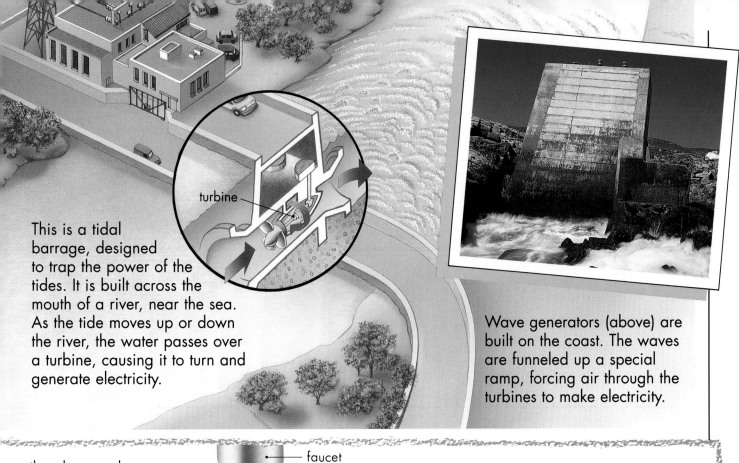

This is a tidal barrage, designed to trap the power of the tides. It is built across the mouth of a river, near the sea. As the tide moves up or down the river, the water passes over a turbine, causing it to turn and generate electricity.

turbine

Wave generators (above) are built on the coast. The waves are funneled up a special ramp, forcing air through the turbines to make electricity.

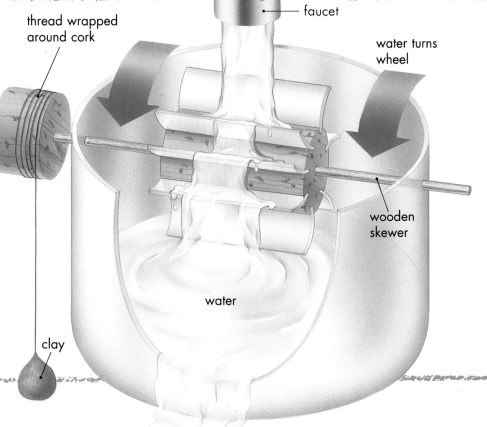

thread wrapped around cork

faucet

water turns wheel

wooden skewer

water

clay

3. Cut away a section of the bottle base as shown. Then pierce two holes just below the rim, one on either side.

4. Cut a wooden skewer in half. Feed each half through a hole and push the sticks into the ends of the cork.

5. Put a second cork on the end of one of the sticks. Tie a length of thread around it and attach a blob of modeling clay. Now put your water-wheel under a faucet. Slowly turn the faucet on and watch your machine lift the weight.

Energy Underground

Hot rocks beneath the Earth's surface have been used as a free source of heat for hundreds of years. Water moving through cracks in the rocks is heated, often to temperatures of up to 660°F (350°C). The hot water can be brought to the surface and used to make electricity. This form of energy is called geothermal energy. It is a very important source of energy in countries such as Iceland and New Zealand.

Hot Rock Power

Geothermal power plants are built in places where there is very hot water in the rocks just below the ground. A pipe is drilled into the rocks to allow steam to escape to the surface, where it is used to drive a turbine and generate electricity for local homes and factories. The waste water is pumped back down into the ground to replace the hot water that has been removed.

Sometimes the water and steam heated by the hot rocks burst out of the ground to form geysers and hot springs. In Iceland, everyone heats their homes with water from hot springs.

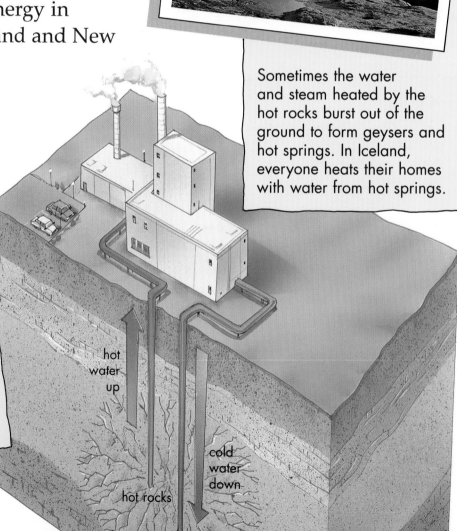

hot water up

cold water down

hot rocks

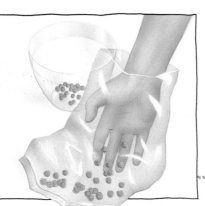

The Wonders of Waste

Garbage could be a cheap source of energy, if only we made more use of it. We have been burying our garbage in holes called landfills for many years. As the waste breaks down it releases a gas called methane. This is often left to escape into the air, but it can be collected and burned to make hot water and electricity for local homes. Or, instead of burying our garbage, we could use it as fuel to make electricity.

In some parts of the world, such as India, animal dung is collected and dried. Then it can be burned on fires for cooking and heating.

Do it yourself

Show that rotting waste gives off a gas.

1. Soak some dried peas or beans in water overnight. Then put them in a clear plastic bag.

2. Squash all the air out of the bag and seal it. Then place the bag somewhere warm and leave it for a week. Now see what has happened. (Throw the bag away without opening it once you have finished the experiment.)

How It Works

The peas or beans soon start to rot as they are broken down by tiny organisms in the air called bacteria. As they rot they give off the gas methane, which causes the bag to blow up.

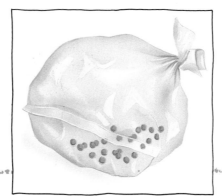

Energy in the Home

Every home uses energy, but what is it needed for? Modern homes are wired so that electricity can be carried to each room, providing power for lights and items such as televisions and toasters. Fuels such as oil, gas, and coal may also be burned in boilers to provide hot water for central heating and for washing. Some equipment is battery-powered. Batteries are stores of energy which contain chemicals that react together to form an electric current. Some batteries can be recharged many times using a power source such as the Sun or electricity.

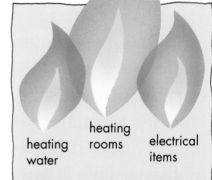

heating water   heating rooms   electrical items

Where Does It Go?

More than half the energy we use at home goes to heat rooms. One-fourth is used to power electrical items and one-fifth is used to heat water for washing.

The modern bedroom is very energy-hungry! We use batteries to power toys and run televisions and radios on electricity.

Eye-Spy

Kitchens use up a lot of energy. Can you figure out why? To help you, count the number of electrical items in your kitchen. How many are there compared with your bedroom?

Do it yourself

Do an energy survey in your home to see how much energy you use.

Write down the gas and electricity meter readings. Then go back three hours later to see by how much they have gone up. Take readings at different times of the day and year to see how the amount of energy you use varies.

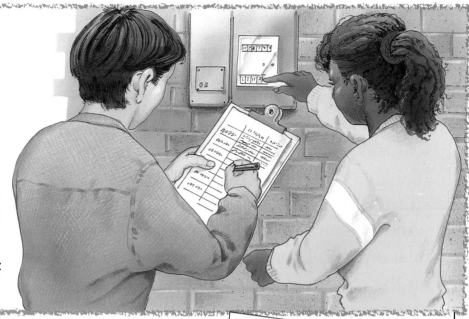

Heating and lighting also use up energy. But we only need them when it is cold or dark outside.

Many people now have computers at home that may be left on for many hours at a time. Computers use up a lot of electricity.

Battery Power

Batteries are a very useful source of energy because they do not have to be wired to the electricity supply. They can be used anywhere to power portable items such as personal stereos. But they do not last very long because the chemicals that power them soon run out.

Tomorrow's Home

The home of the future may look very different from the ones we live in today. There will be many energy-saving features, as well as ways of making use of free energy sources such as the Sun. The sunny side of the house will have large windows and maybe a sun porch to trap heat energy. There will be solar panels on the roof to trap sunlight, and water pipes underground will pick up heat from the soil.

This house has been designed to use energy as efficiently as possible and to make the most use of free energy sources.

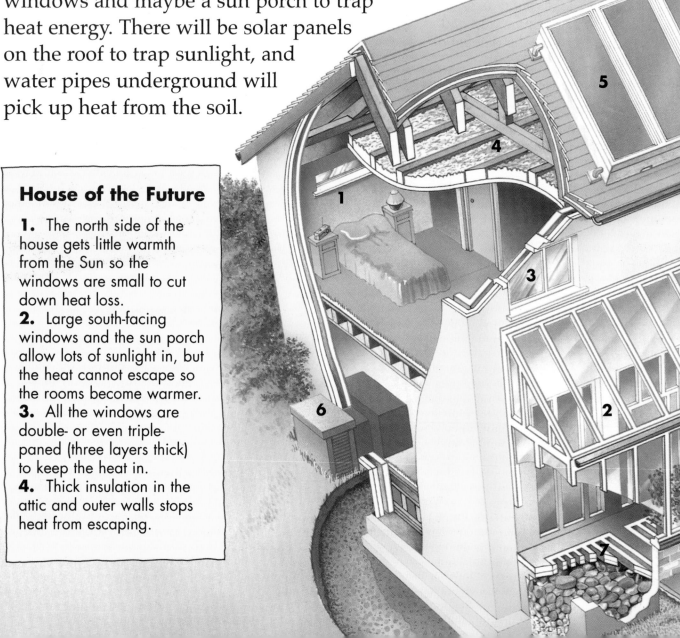

House of the Future

1. The north side of the house gets little warmth from the Sun so the windows are small to cut down heat loss.

2. Large south-facing windows and the sun porch allow lots of sunlight in, but the heat cannot escape so the rooms become warmer.

3. All the windows are double- or even triple-paned (three layers thick) to keep the heat in.

4. Thick insulation in the attic and outer walls stops heat from escaping.

This house in Switzerland has special solar tiles to replace the normal roof tiles. If we use solar power more widely (even in cloudy areas) there will be less need to build new power plants.

Electric cars may be more common in the future. Solar energy could be used to make electricity to recharge the car.

5. Solar panels on the roof trap heat energy and use it to provide the house with plenty of hot water.

6. A heat exchanger pumps water through underground pipes. In winter it is used to absorb heat from the ground to warm the house. In summer it loses heat into the ground to keep the house cool.

7. A heat collector in the ground absorbs heat from the soil which is used to warm the sun porch.

8. The garage is fitted with a car recharger so the car's battery can be recharged overnight.

Save It!

We all use too much energy. If we reduce the amount we use each day we will create less pollution and our fossil fuels will last longer. There are many ways of saving energy in the home. Houses can be built with better "insulation" to stop heat escaping through the walls and roof. Low-energy light bulbs are widely available, and many electrical goods now carry labels telling us how much energy they use so we can buy the most efficient.

Eye-Spy

Does your family use low-energy light bulbs? They last about eight times as long as ordinary light bulbs and use about one-fourth of the electricity.

Do it yourself

Insulation is used to stop heat escaping. Do this simple experiment to see which materials hold heat the longest.

Wrap four bottles in different materials as shown and pour an equal amount of hot water (from the hot faucet) into each one. Take the temperature of the water in each bottle, then take it again after 5 minutes, 10 minutes, and 20 minutes. Which material gives the best insulation? Which would you wear to keep warm?

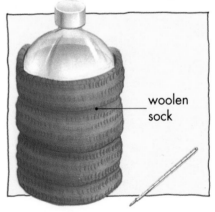

newspaper

woolen sock

aluminum foil

thermometer

plastic bag

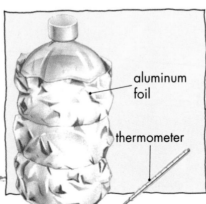

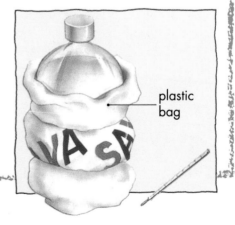

BATTERIES, BULBS, AND WIRES

An Electric World

It's hard to imagine what life was like without electricity — no electric lights, no televisions, no computers. Yet only one hundred years ago hardly any of these things existed. Scientists could make electricity with a battery or with magnets and wires, but the first electric light bulb had only just been invented. Most people still used coal and gas to heat and light their homes.

Eye-Spy

List ten things around your home that use electricity, then challenge an adult to add ten more things to your list.

In this book you'll also read about magnets. Can you think of any places where magnets are used? Perhaps you use magnets to attach messages or postcards to the door of your refrigerator.

The appliances shown below use *current* electricity. There is also a *static* electricity (see next page).

Do it yourself

Discover static electricity!

Rub a balloon against your sweater. This will make static electricity build up on the balloon's plastic skin. Then hold the balloon against a wall and remove your hand — the static electricity should make the balloon cling there.

Hint: Experiments with static electricity work best on a dry day.

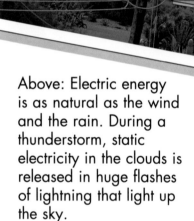

Above: Electric energy is as natural as the wind and the rain. During a thunderstorm, static electricity in the clouds is released in huge flashes of lightning that light up the sky.

rub on a sweater — wool and nylon work well

WARNING!

The electric wires in your home are joined to the electricity supply from a power plant. They carry a huge amount of electricity and are very dangerous. So:
- **Never** use the main electricity supply for your experiments.
- **Never** go near electric pylons or cables like the ones in the photograph above.

A First Look at Magnets

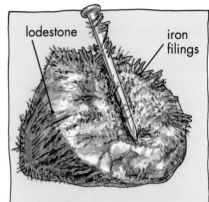

lodestone

iron filings

Do you have any magnets? What shape are they? Magnets come in all shapes and sizes but they all pull and push with an invisible force. And all magnets pull, or attract, some things but not others. For example, all magnets attract the metal iron. So if you use a magnet to pick up pins, it will only attract them if they contain iron.

Natural Magnets

The black rock called lodestone is a natural magnet. Pieces of the rock attract things made of iron, like this iron nail and the small iron filings. Another name for lodestone is magnetite.

Do it yourself

Test different materials, such as nails, paper clips, pins, pencils, and coins, to see whether they are magnetic. You should be able to feel the magnet's "pull" when it attracts something.

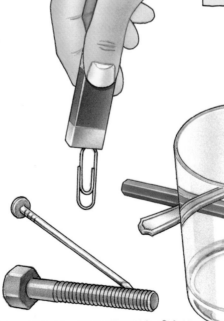

Pull and Push

The two poles of a magnet are called the north pole and the south pole. This is because when a magnet swings freely it always settles with its north pole pointing toward Earth's North Pole, and its south pole pointing south. Both poles of a magnet attract iron, but the poles of different magnets do not always attract or pull toward each other. Sometimes, the poles repel each other, or push apart.

Magnet Laws

In the experiment below, you've discovered the laws of magnets. A south pole always repels a south pole and a north pole always repels a north pole. But a north pole always attracts a south pole and a south pole always attracts a north pole.

Scientists say:
Like poles repel and unlike poles attract.

Hint: Some magnets have "north" and "south" labeled on them. If your magnets do not have labels, look for a tiny dent at one end. That end is the magnet's north pole.

Do it yourself

Test the force between the poles of two bar magnets.

Tape one of the magnets to a cork and float it on some water. Slowly bring the north pole of the second magnet toward the south pole of the floating magnet to see what happens. Make a chart like the one below and try the other combinations.

Poles	Attract or Repel
south/north	
south/south	
north/north	
north/south	

slice of cork

The Pull of the Earth

Did you know that the whole Earth is magnetic? That's why a magnetic compass needle always points in the same direction — the poles of the compass needle are attracted to the Earth's North and South Poles. It's as if the Earth had a huge bar magnet inside. Scientists believe that this magnetism comes from the red-hot melted iron deep inside the Earth.

Getting Home

Homing pigeons can sense the Earth's magnetism. They're able to find their way home after they have been released hundreds of miles away.

Magnetic Flip

Scientists have studied the magnetism in ancient rocks. They've found that every so often the Earth's magnetic North and South Poles swap places. No one knows why this happens, or when it will happen next.

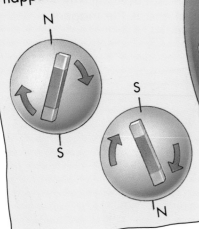

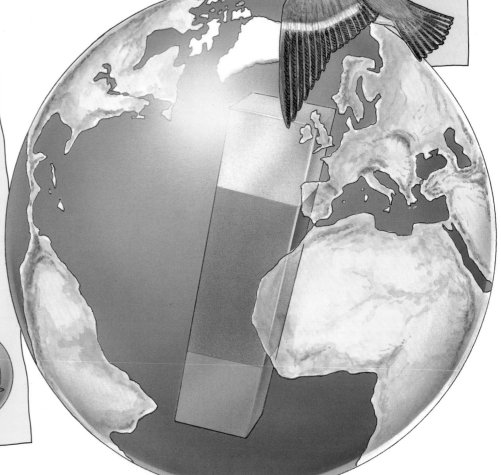

Do it yourself

A compass needle swings freely and always settles down pointing north-south. To make your own compass, you'll need a magnet, a steel needle, a piece of cork, and a shallow dish.

1. Make the needle magnetic by stroking it with a magnet at least 50 times—in one direction only.

2. Place the needle on the cork and float it in a dish filled with water.

3. When the needle settles down, watch which direction it points in. Check the direction with a real pocket compass and label it North.

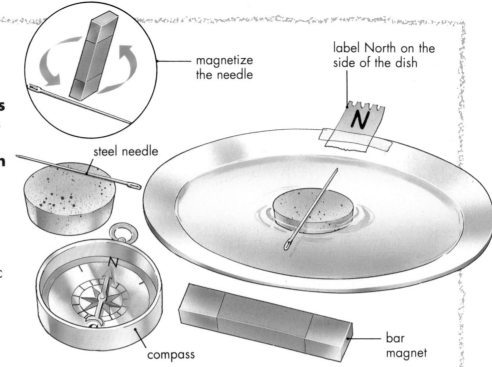

magnetize the needle

steel needle

label North on the side of the dish

compass

bar magnet

Using a Compass

To use a compass, place the compass on a map and turn the map around until the North arrow points in the same direction as the compass needle.

False Readings!

If you hold an iron nail near a compass needle, the needle will twist around as it's attracted to the iron. So don't hold a compass close to something made of iron — like a belt buckle — or you'll get a false reading!

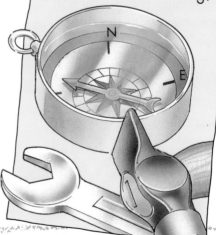

Magnets at Work

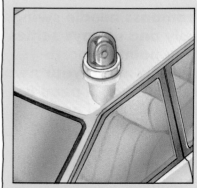

Magnets are used to make compasses, and some doors have bar magnets fastened to them to hold them shut. In space, where things do not have any weight, astronauts use magnets to hold things like toothbrushes onto the walls of their spacecraft to stop them floating around. Magnets are also used with electricity to make electric motors work. You can read more about how magnets and electricity are linked on page **52**.

A powerful magnet can hold a warning light to the roof of a police car or a doctor's car.

Magnetic Sorting

Food cans are usually made from steel and soda cans from aluminum. The two metals must be separated before they are melted down and recycled. As steel is attracted by magnets and aluminum is not, you can sort them with a magnet.

Cassette and videotapes use magnetism to record sounds and pictures. The tape is coated with a special magnetic material. Sounds or images are then recorded on to the tape as magnetic patterns.

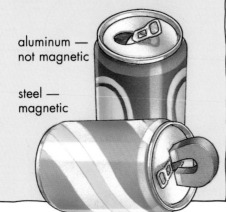

aluminum —
not magnetic

steel —
magnetic

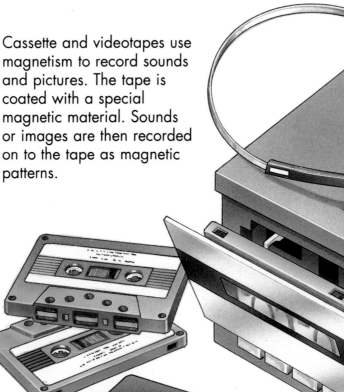

Do it yourself

Here are ideas for two games you can make using magnets.

Fish (2 - 6 Players)

Tie small horseshoe magnets to the ends of the bamboo sticks (one for each player). Cut out the plastic fish and write scores on each with a waterproof marker. Attach metal paper clips to the fish. Fill a deep bowl with water and drop in the fish so the numbers are face down.

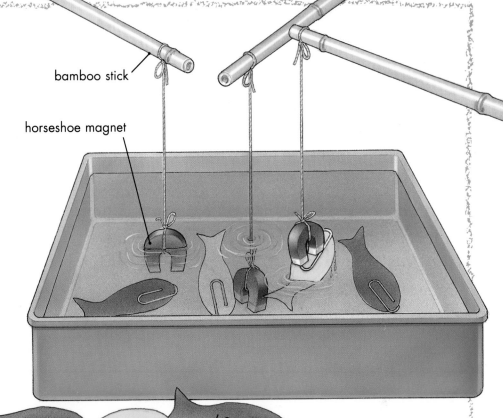

bamboo stick

horseshoe magnet

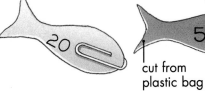

20

5   15   10

cut from plastic bag

metal paper clip

Roundup (2 Players)

Make sheep and sheep pens from cardboard, as shown. Tape a small round magnet to the end of each ruler.

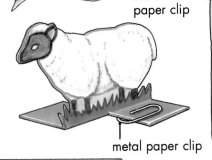

metal paper clip

tray or thin wooden board

tape down

small round magnet

How To Play Fish

The players should stand at equal distances from the bowl. Shout "Go" and start fishing. At the end of the game, the player with the most points wins.

How To Play Roundup

Round up the sheep and put them in your pen. (You can't take sheep out of the other player's pen.) The one with the most sheep wins.

41

Getting Started

The best way to learn about electricity is to experiment with it. But remember — never touch the electricity supply in your home. It can kill.

To get started, collect all the things you'll need and keep them in a box. For some activities, you'll need a buzzer and a motor. You can buy these quite cheaply from a hobby store or an electrical store.

Basic Experiment Kit

1. Batteries (see next page)
2. Balsa wood, or cork pieces
3. Small screwdriver
4. Plastic-coated wire
5. Bulbs and bulb holders
6. Metal paper clips and thumbtacks
7. Tape

Preparing Wire

Most wires come with a plastic coating. To join the wire to a bulb holder or to a paper clip, you must ask an adult to help you strip some of the plastic from the end so you can see the metal. Follow stages 1 to 4 which show you how to do this.

Wires can also be attached to alligator clips (right) which are then covered with plastic cases.

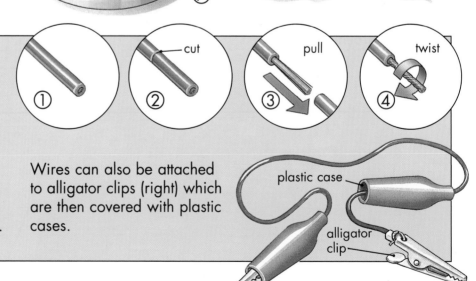

cut

pull

twist

plastic case

alligator clip

Choosing Batteries

All batteries have two terminals — a positive (+) and a negative (–). Look on the outside of your batteries to see how many volts they have.

The simplest batteries are 1.5V (one and a half volts). You can also buy 4.5V or 9V batteries. A 4.5V battery has three 1.5V cells inside it. A 9V battery has six 1.5V cells. Use 1.5V or 4.5V batteries for the experiments in this book.

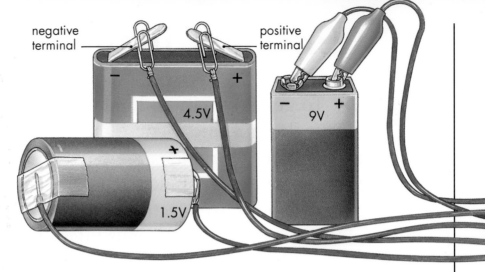

negative terminal
positive terminal
4.5V
9V
1.5V

Join the wires and batteries with tape, metal paper clips, or alligator clips. Or use a battery holder.

Whichever method you use, make sure that the metal parts touch tightly, or your experiments won't work.

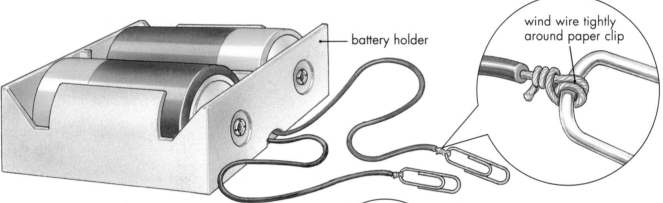

battery holder

wind wire tightly around paper clip

Bulbs and Bulb Holders

Bulbs are made to work with a certain number of volts. This number is printed on the base of the bulb. Always use a bulb that is the same number of volts, or more volts, than your battery.

Gently screw the bulb into the holder, then screw the stripped wire under each of the holder's terminals, as shown on the right.

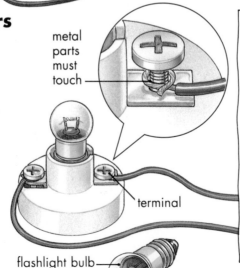

metal parts must touch

terminal

flashlight bulb

WARNING!

- **Never** use the main electricity supply for your experiments. It can kill.
- **Never** open a battery. The chemicals inside are dangerous.
- **Always** follow the directions carefully when performing these experiments.

Simple Circuits

To get electricity to light a bulb, it must flow around a complete path, or circuit. The battery provides the power. It pushes an electric current along the wires and through the bulb. An electric circuit works a little like the chain on your bike. When you push the pedals, your power is carried by the chain to the back wheel. If the chain breaks, the wheel won't turn. If an electric circuit is broken, the current stops flowing and the light goes out.

Wires at Work

Connecting the tiny electric circuits in a television is very complicated. Every circuit must be complete or the TV set won't work.

Making a Circuit

Cut two lengths of wire and strip both ends (see page 42). Connect each wire to the battery and bulb holder as shown. You can use tape, paper clips, or alligator clips, as used here.

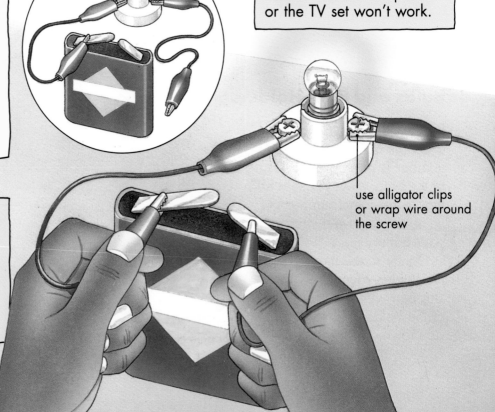

broken circuit

use alligator clips or wrap wire around the screw

How It Works

The battery pushes an electric current around the circuit. The current heats the fine wire in the bulb, so it glows.

Do it yourself

Switches are useful because you can decide whether or not you want the electricity to flow. Make this simple switch to add to your circuit.

1. Take one of the wires off the bulb holder and wrap the end tightly around a thumbtack.

2. Push the tack through the end of a paper clip and into a piece of balsa wood.

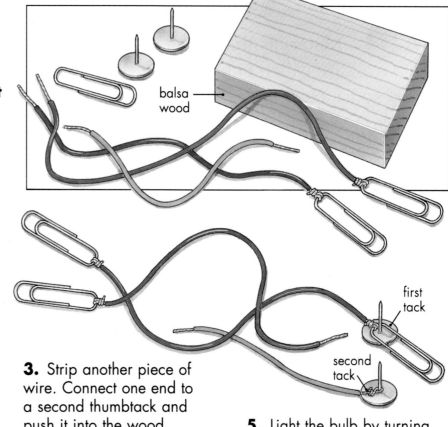

balsa wood

first tack

second tack

3. Strip another piece of wire. Connect one end to a second thumbtack and push it into the wood.

4. Connect the free end of the new wire to the free screw on the bulb holder.

5. Light the bulb by turning the paper clip so that it touches both tacks. Move the second thumbtack if the paper clip won't reach.

OFF

ON

How It Works

When the switch is on, there's a complete circuit for the electricity to flow around, so the bulb lights up. When it's off, there's a break in the circuit, so the electricity can't flow and the bulb won't light.

An Electric Test

Materials that carry electricity well are called conductors. Metal is a good conductor of electricity. Things that don't carry electricity are called insulators. Plastic is an insulator. Many electrical wires are covered in plastic, for safety.

Do it yourself

Test a collection of materials to see whether they're conductors or insulators.

1. Take the switch out of your circuit so that you are left with two bare wires. If you touch the two wires together you will complete the circuit and the bulb will glow.

2. Touch the material to be tested with both wires. The bulb will light if the material conducts electricity. A metal nail, for example, will complete the circuit, lighting up the bulb.

3. Make a note of your results.

object to be tested

Conductors

Insulators

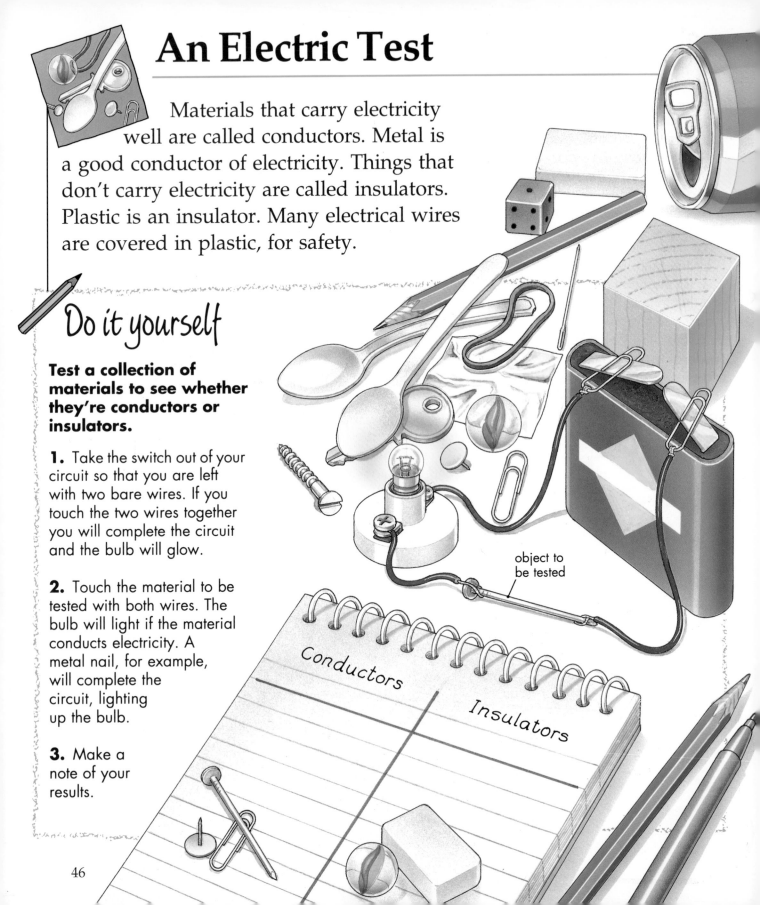

Three Circuit Projects

Here are three circuit projects for you to try — a burglar alarm, a Morse code key, and a test of skill. For each of the projects you'll need to make a simple circuit and a special sort of switch.

How It Works

When someone steps on them, the two pieces of cardboard touch. As they are wrapped in metal foil, they form a complete circuit, so the buzzer goes off or the bulb lights up.

Do it yourself

To make a burglar alarm, you will need a battery and wires, a buzzer, two plastic straws, aluminum foil, and some cardboard.

1. Cut out two pieces of cardboard. Tape foil around them and make a hole in one end of each piece.

2. Tape the cardboard pieces together with straws in between, so that they are close but do not touch. Attach one wire to each piece of cardboard as shown.

3. Wire your cardboard switch in a circuit with the battery and buzzer. Use long wires so that you can hide your alarm around a corner or even in another room. Use a bulb instead of a buzzer for a silent alarm.

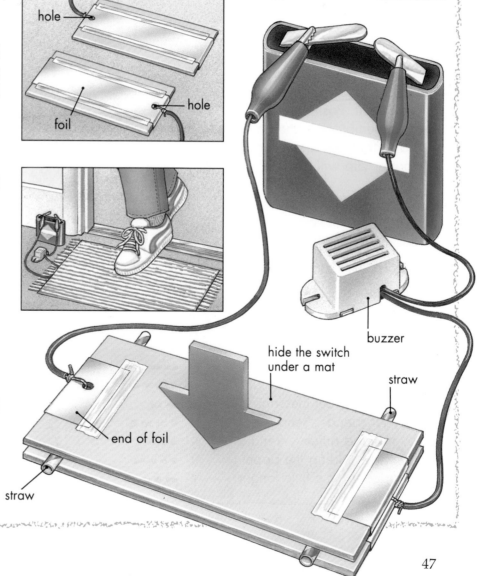

hole

foil

hole

buzzer

hide the switch under a mat

straw

end of foil

straw

47

Do it yourself

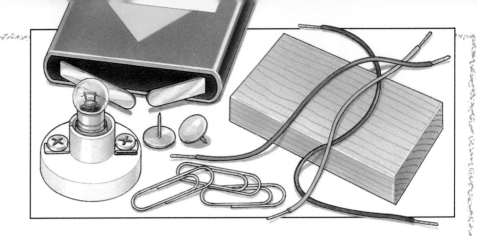

The first messages sent by electricity were tapped out in a code of dots and dashes called Morse code. Make your own Morse code key.

1. Open out a small paper clip and bend one end up. You can tape a plastic button over the raised end to make it easier to use.

2. Pin the paper clip to a piece of balsa wood with a thumbtack and wire the switch into a circuit. Position the second thumbtack in the balsa wood so that the raised end of the paper clip will touch it.

When you press down the paper clip it will complete the circuit, lighting up the bulb or working the buzzer.

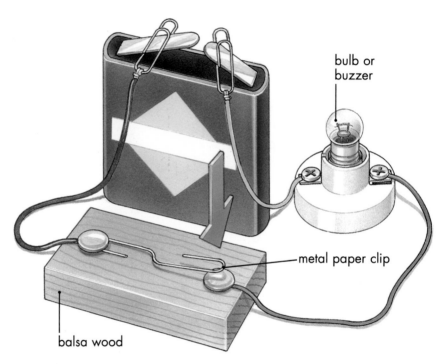

bulb or buzzer

metal paper clip

balsa wood

Morse Code

The International Morse code is shown on the right. Try tapping out messages to your friends. Send a dot by tapping quickly. Send a dash by holding the paper clip down for a little longer.

A	•—	B	—•••	C	—•—•
D	—••	E	•	F	••—•
G	——•	H	••••	I	••
J	•———	K	—•—	L	•—••
M	——	N	—•	O	———
P	•——•	Q	——•—	R	•—•
S	•••	T	—	U	••—
V	•••—	W	•——	X	—••—
Y	—•——	Z	——••		

Do it yourself

Try this test of skill. Is your hand steady enough to take the loop from one end of the wire to the other without lighting a bulb or setting off a buzzer?

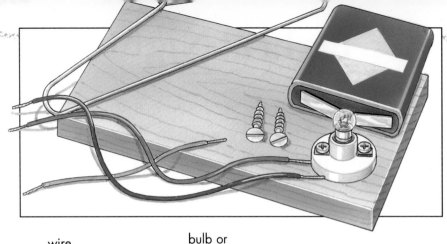

wire coathanger

bulb or buzzer

third wire

screw wire into wood

bend into loop

wooden board

first wire

second wire

How It Works

If the looped wire touches the curved wire, the circuit will be completed so the bulb will light up or the buzzer will buzz.

1. Ask an adult to help you bend a wire coathanger into an interesting curved shape and screw the wire to a wooden board.

2. Bend the end of a shorter piece of coathanger wire into a small loop around the curvy wire on the board.

3. Attach one end of the first piece of stripped wire to the bottom of the short looped coathanger wire and the other end to the battery terminal.

4. Connect the second wire from the battery to the bulb holder and the third wire from the bulb holder to one end of the curved coathanger wire.

Light at Night

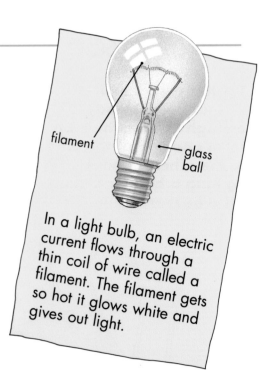

Electric lights have completely changed the way we live. We can do things at night almost as if it were still day. We can play football by floodlight and go shopping in brightly-lit shopping malls. Motorists can drive at night using car headlights, and streetlights show us the road. The centers of some big cities, like Hong Kong below, now have so many lights that astronauts can see them from space.

In a light bulb, an electric current flows through a thin coil of wire called a filament. The filament gets so hot it glows white and gives out light.

How Light Bulbs Work

Touch the ends of two wires from a battery to a thread of fine steel wool and see how the wool glows as it is heated. When things burn, they need oxygen gas from the air. Light bulbs don't contain any oxygen, so the filament glows but does not burn away.

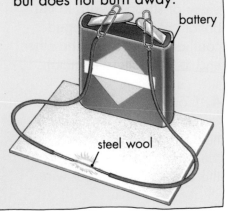

Do it yourself

Suppose you want to light two bulbs from just one battery. There are two ways that you can wire up the circuit — as a series circuit or as a parallel circuit.

The two types of circuit are shown below. Wire up both kinds so that you can compare them.

The bulbs in the parallel circuit will glow more brightly than those in the series circuit.

Try taking one of the bulbs out of its holder in each circuit to see what happens to the other bulb.

Eye-Spy

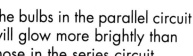

Outdoor Christmas lights are usually wired as a parallel circuit so if one goes out, the rest stay alight. Indoor lights are usually wired as a series circuit, which is safer.

series circuit — bulbs are wired as one single circuit

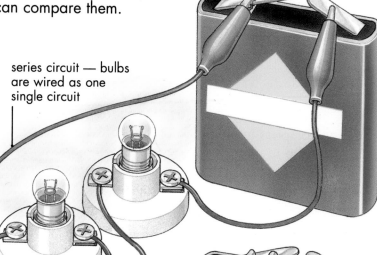

parallel circuit — bulbs are wired as a double circuit

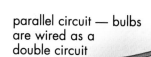

How It Works

The electricity can only flow one way in a series circuit. If you remove a bulb the circuit will be broken and the other bulb will go out.

In a parallel circuit, each bulb is wired in its own circuit. So if you remove a bulb, the electricity can still flow around the circuit and the other bulb will stay alight.

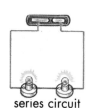

parallel circuit

series circuit

Magnetic Links

In 1820, a scientist called Hans Oersted was experimenting with an electric circuit when he suddenly noticed that a compass needle near the wires moved when he switched the electricity on and off. He had made an important discovery — that an electric current produces magnetism.

Do it yourself

Try repeating Oersted's famous experiment.

1. Wrap a length of wire around a cardboard tube as shown. (This makes the magnetism stronger.) Then connect the wire to a battery and a switch.

2. Slide a small compass into the middle of the tube.

3. Switch the electric circuit on and off and watch what happens to the compass needle.

In this MAGLEV (magnetic levitation) train, electro-magnets in the train are repelled by magnetism in the track, making the train float along.

How It Works

When you switch on the circuit the electricity produces magnetism all around the wire. This attracts the compass needle and makes it swing. When the circuit is off, there is no magnetism produced so the needle goes back to its north-south position.

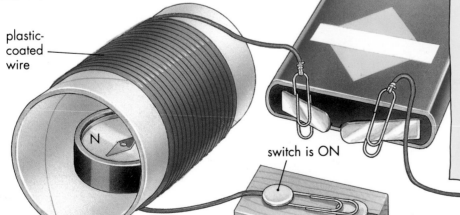

plastic-coated wire

N

switch is ON

Do it yourself

A magnet that works by electricity is called an electromagnet. Make an electromagnet with a long iron nail, wire, a battery, and a switch.

1. Wind the wire around the nail, as shown. This will become your electromagnet.

2. Wire up the electromagnet in a circuit with the battery and the switch.

3. Switch on the circuit and test the magnet to see if it will pick up paper clips or pins.

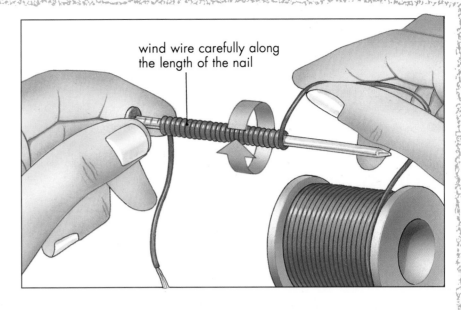

wind wire carefully along the length of the nail

The electric current in the coil of wire makes the tiny magnets inside the iron nail line up, turning the nail itself into a magnet.

More Things to Try

Try bringing one end of the electromagnet toward a compass needle to see whether the needle is attracted or repelled. Then try the same thing with the other end of the magnet.

Now change the wires around on your battery and try the same thing again. Your results should now be the other way around.

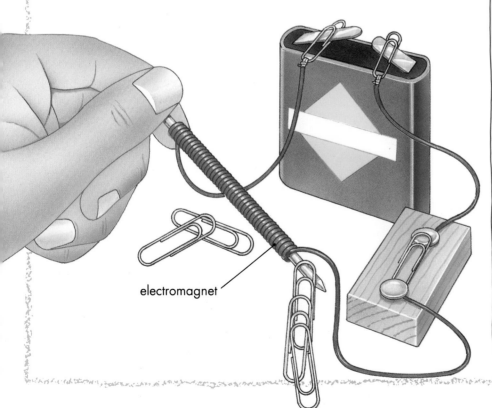

electromagnet

Electric Sounds

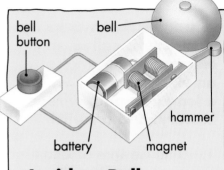

When you play a cassette tape or listen to the radio, you are hearing sounds that have been made with electricity. Buzzers, bells, and loudspeakers also turn electricity into sound.

Telephones work in a similar way. They change the sounds of our voices into electricity. These electric signals can be carried along wires to another phone, or beamed by satellite to the other side of the world.

Inside a Bell

A doorbell uses electricity to make a hammer strike a bell. When you press the bell button, a magnet is turned on. This makes the metal hammer strike against the bell.

When you pick up the receiver, the small loudspeaker in the earpiece turns the electric signals into sound waves which are then picked up by your ear.

First Telephone Call

Imagine life without telephones! Alexander Graham Bell invented the telephone in 1876. The first words he spoke were to his assistant. He said, "Mr. Watson, come here, I want you."

small loudspeaker

loudspeaker

microphone

Do it yourself

Discover how electric signals are turned back into sounds. You'll need an old transistor radio earpiece or loudspeaker, and a battery.

The wires of old radio earpieces usually have two strands. Carefully separate the strands and touch the end of one strand to one battery terminal and the end of the other strand to the other battery terminal. What do you hear?

If you have one, try this same experiment with an old radio loudspeaker. You should be able to see and feel the loudspeaker cone move slightly when the battery is connected.

An earpiece also makes a good *static* electricity detector. Try rubbing a balloon with some wool and then touch the balloon with the earpiece wires.

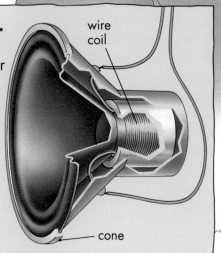

Inside a Loudspeaker

In a radio, it's the loudspeaker that makes sounds. Inside, there's a magnet and a coil of wire. When an electric current flows through the coil, it's pushed back and forth by the magnet. The coil makes the cone move backward and forward too, producing sounds.

wire coil

cone

Electric Motors

Another important discovery to do with electricity and magnetism was made in 1821 by a scientist called Michael Faraday. He found out that magnetism from an electric current can be used to make electric motors turn.

Compared to gasoline engines, electric motors are clean and quiet. It's possible that in the future we may have electric cars which could help to keep our cities cleaner and cause less pollution.

Eye-Spy

Look out for things around your home that use electric motors. (Don't turn anything on without asking first.)

drill

razor

hairdryer

Turning Motors

Buy a cheap electric motor from a hobby store to try this experiment. Attach a block from a construction kit to the motor's spindle so you can see which way the motor turns.

Connect the motor to some batteries. See which way the motor turns and how fast it goes. Now try connecting the wires the other way around. The spindle should now turn in the opposite direction.

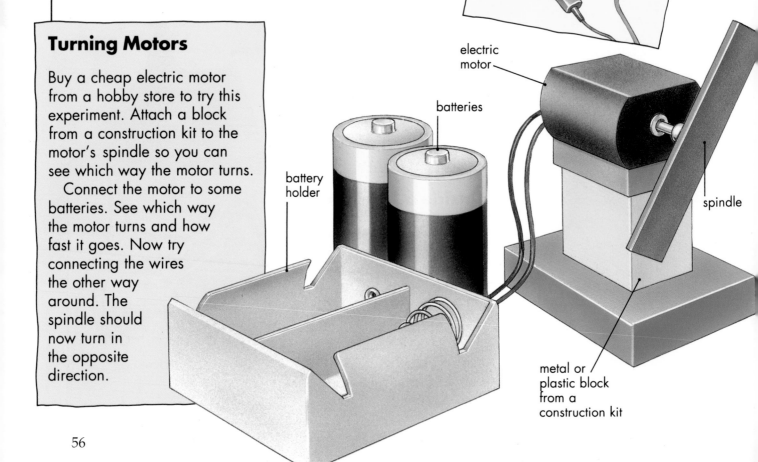

electric motor

batteries

battery holder

spindle

metal or plastic block from a construction kit

Do it yourself

Try building this electric winch.

1. Ask an adult to help you cut three pieces of wood to the shapes shown on the right and nail them together.

2. Slide two empty spools onto a dowel and glue them together. Make sure that the spools can turn freely.

3. Hook a rubber band over one of the spools and slide the dowel through the holes in the side pieces. Then glue the dowel firmly in place.

4. Attach the electric motor to the base board with tape.

5. Connect the motor to a battery and switch.

6. Glue the end of a piece of string to the second spool and wind the string around it several times. Attach a load to the free end of the string.

When you turn on the switch, the motor should turn the spools, winding in the string and load.

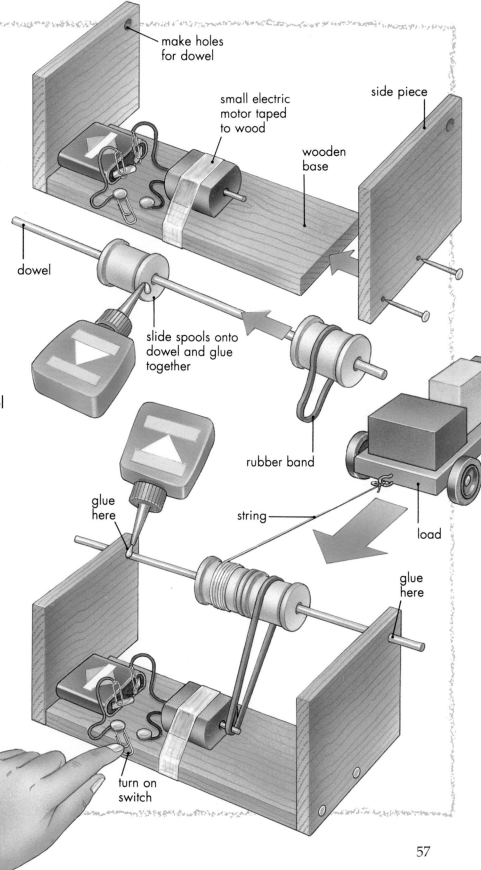

make holes for dowel

small electric motor taped to wood

side piece

wooden base

dowel

slide spools onto dowel and glue together

rubber band

glue here

string

load

glue here

glue here

turn on switch

Solar Power

Solar cells turn light from the Sun into electricity. Many pocket calculators are powered by sunlight. There have also been experiments with solar-powered cars (right) and planes, but they need a sunny climate to work well. Solar-powered machines do not cause pollution.

Moving Magnets

Some bicycle lamps use a simple dynamo to make an electric current. The turning wheel moves a magnet inside a wire coil, making the light come on. Today, most bicycle lamps work with batteries.

dynamo

Animal Electricity

Some fish can make their own electric currents. Catfish use electricity to feel their way along the bottom of a stream or river. Electric eels stun their prey with an electric shock — they can produce an electric shock that is powerful enough to knock down a person.

SOUND AND LIGHT

Thunder and Lightning

Have you ever been caught in a thunderstorm? First you see a flash of lightning, then you hear a crash of thunder. The sky is filled with light and sound.

Lightning flashes are huge sparks of electricity. They are so powerful they can be seen a long way from a storm. Light travels very fast, so we see the flash of light in the same second that it is made. But sound travels more slowly. It may be several seconds before the sound of a thunderclap reaches our ears.

The Vikings believed that thunder was the sound of their god, Odin, hammering his sword ready for war.

How Far Is the Storm?

Light travels a million times faster than sound, so it arrives almost instantly. But sound takes about 5 seconds to travel 1 mile.

You can work out how far a thunderstorm is from you by timing the number of seconds between seeing a lightning flash and hearing the roll of thunder.

If you count $2\frac{1}{2}$ seconds, then the storm is half a mile away, 5 seconds means that it is 1 mile away, 10 seconds 2 miles, and so on.

Eye-Spy

Look out for light arriving before you hear sound. For example, next time you go to a firework display, see if you can see the rockets exploding before you hear the bangs.

The giant sparks of electricity given off by lightning can strike tall trees and set them on fire. So **never** shelter under a tree during a thunderstorm.

In cities, many tall buildings have lightning rods running down their sides. These metal rods carry the electricity safely down the buildings into the ground.

61

Sound Waves

If you flick the end of a rope up and down, the "flick" travels along the rope like a wave — the section of rope in your hand passes the movement on to the next section, which passes it on again, and so on. This is how sound travels through the air. When you burst a balloon, the escaping air gives a sudden push to the air around it. This push is passed on through the air like the wave traveling along the rope and we hear the loud bang, or pop, when the sound wave reaches our ears.

Making a Bang

Bursting an air-filled paper bag forces the air trapped inside the bag through the hole in the paper. This sends a powerful sound wave through the air that reaches our ears as a loud bang.

Tie a rope to a tree or to a lamppost and flick the free end up and down to see how waves move along the rope.

Passing It On

Set up a row of dominoes, spacing them fairly close together. Now knock the first one over and watch how the wave travels down the line.

Do it yourself

Build a sound cannon so you can see a sound wave make a candle flicker. You will need a cardboard tube, some plastic, scissors, tape, a small candle, a saucer, and some sand.

1. Stretch the pieces of plastic tightly across each end of the cardboard tube and tape them firmly in place.

2. Make a small hole in the middle of the plastic at one end of the tube.

tape firmly in place or use rubber bands

plastic cut from plastic bag

3. Put some sand in the saucer and stand the candle upright in it. Ask an adult to light the candle for you.

4. Hold the end of the tube with the hole in it about an inch away from the flame.

5. Tap the other end of the tube with your finger. Watch what happens to the flame.

Noisiest Explosion

When the Indonesian island of Krakatoa exploded in 1883, the sound wave was heard in Australia, 2,500 miles away.

How It Works

When you tap the plastic, you make a sound wave that travels down the tube and out of the hole at the end. The wave can be strong enough to blow out the candle flame.

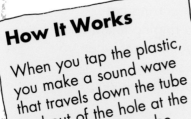
candle

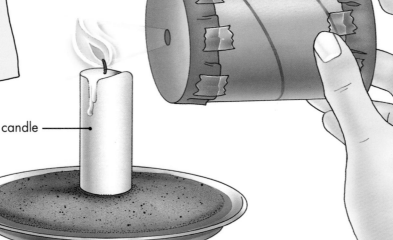
saucer filled with sand or soil

Feeling Sound

If you bend the end of a ruler over the edge of a table and then let it go, the ruler will move up and down. When something moves quickly back and forth like this, we say that it is vibrating.

Try changing the length of the ruler on the table. The shorter the length over the edge, the quicker the vibrations and the higher the sound. We call the number of sound waves a second, the *frequency* of the waves.

Nearly every sound you hear is made by something vibrating.

Feeling Vibrations

When something is making a steady sound it must be vibrating to push the air around it back and forth. If you hold your hand against things making sounds you can usually feel the vibrations. Here are some things to test:
- a purring cat
- a ringing telephone
- your throat when you are singing
- a radio playing loud music

Seeing Vibrations

We cannot see sound waves, but sometimes we can see the vibrations that make sounds. Sprinkle a few grains of uncooked rice on some paper, lay it over a radio and watch the rice jump!

turn up sound

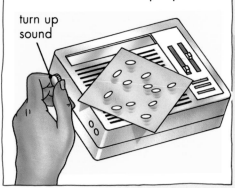

press this end down firmly

If you stretch a rubber band between your fingers and twang it, it vibrates and makes a quiet sound. The sound isn't very loud because the band is small and it can only push a small amount of air. To make the sound louder we must amplify it. In other words, we must make the vibrations of the elastic band push more air to and fro.

Do it yourself

Make a sound amplifier. You will need a large plastic mixing bowl, a sheet of plastic cut from a plastic bag, tape, scissors, and two rubber bands.

1. Stretch the plastic tightly over the top of the bowl, like the skin of a drum. Secure the plastic with a rubber band and tape.

2. Tape the other rubber band to the middle of the plastic.

3. Now stretch the loose band and twang it.

How It Works

When the band vibrates it makes the stretched plastic vibrate. Because the plastic sheet is much bigger than the elastic band, it pushes a lot more air and amplifies the sound. That's why a jack-hammer makes a very loud noise — it vibrates the ground around it.

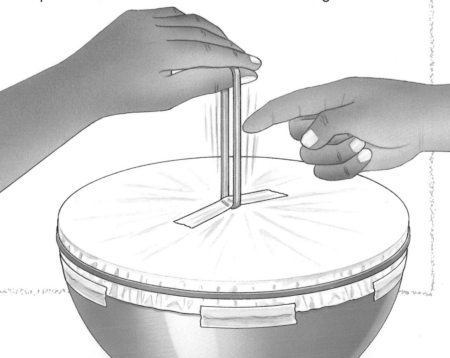

Making Music

All musical instruments use vibrations to make sounds. Stringed instruments, like guitars, have stretched strings that vibrate when they are plucked or strummed. Wind instruments, like recorders or clarinets, make vibrations when the musician blows down the tube. Percussion instruments, like drums, triangles, and cymbals, are usually played by hitting or tapping them to make them vibrate.

Moving Air

Because a triangle only moves a small amount of air, it makes a quiet sound. The cymbals are bigger and move a lot more air. So they make a loud sound when they are crashed together.

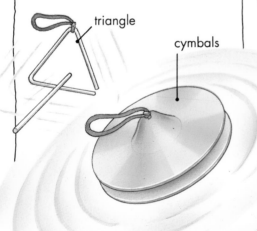

triangle

cymbals

body vibrates, amplifying the sound

sound hole

body

strings

👁 Eye-Spy

When you see an orchestra playing, see if you can pick out the sounds of different instruments.

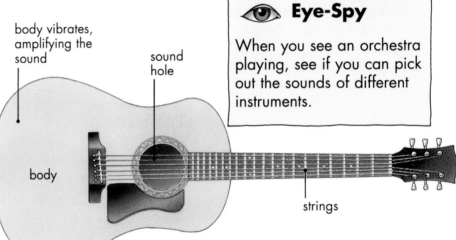

funnel-shape amplifies the sound

The trumpet is a brass instrument. The player makes sounds by vibrating her lips.

Do it yourself

Make your own musical instruments.

1. Make a trumpet with a short piece of hose and a funnel. When you blow into it, try to vibrate your lips — it takes lots of practice to get a clear note.

2. Try blowing over the top of an empty bottle. If you fill several bottles with different amounts of water, you can get high and low notes. Or you could blow sharply over a pen top to make a high, piercing whistle.

3. Make a rich, deep note with a string bass like the one in the picture. Ask an adult to drill a hole in one end of the pole so you can thread string through it. Knot the string tightly under the top of the box and pluck it. Cut a hole in the box to make the sound louder.

4. Tap small cans, large pans, big, empty boxes, or glass jars with pens, spoons, or anything else you can find. Some things will make dull sounds that fade quickly. Others vibrate for longer and make bright sounds that ring on.

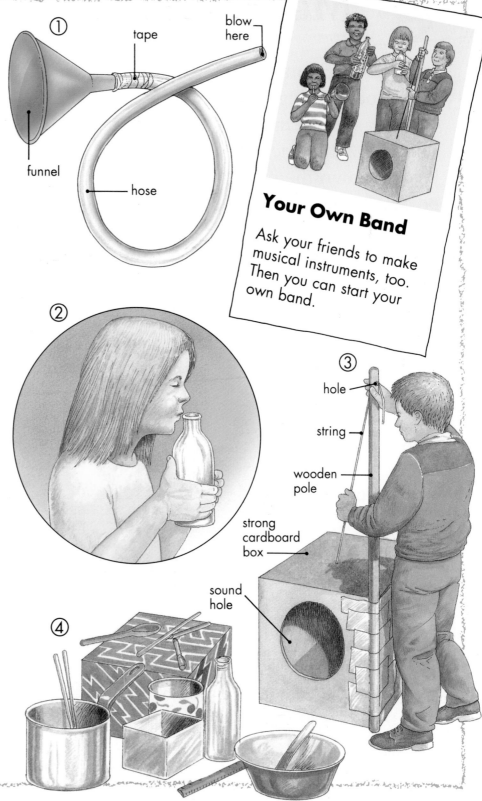

① tape · blow here · funnel · hose

Your Own Band

Ask your friends to make musical instruments, too. Then you can start your own band.

②

③ hole · string · wooden pole · strong cardboard box · sound hole

④

Moving Sound

Sound can travel through other things besides air. Test this out by asking a friend to tap some metal railings with a stick while you stand farther down the railings. You should be able to hear the sound, but if you put your ear close to the metal the sound will be a lot louder.

Sound also travels well through water. In fact, sound travels five times faster through water than it does through air.

👁 Eye-Spy

Next time you swim in the ocean or a pool, listen to how different everything sounds underwater. (Only try this if you can swim really well!)

Do it yourself

Make a yogurt container telephone to hear sounds travel along string.

yogurt container

string (about 10 feet long)

knot

1. Ask an adult to help you make a small hole in the bottom of each container.

2. Thread the ends of the string through each hole and knot them. Hold one of the containers to your ear while a friend speaks into the other. Remember to keep the string tightly stretched.

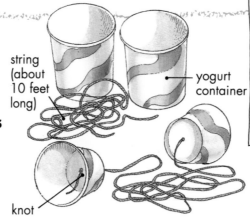

How It Works

Your friend's voice makes the bottom of his or her container vibrate. This makes the string vibrate, too. The sound waves travel along the string, making the bottom of your container vibrate so that you hear your friend's voice.

Bouncing Sound

If you shout when you are standing in a tunnel or in a large, empty room, the sound made by your voice will hit the walls and bounce back. This reflected sound is called an echo. Echoes are louder when they hit a hard barrier, like the walls of a tunnel. Soft materials, like carpets and drapes, absorb or soak up sound. That's why you will hear an echo in an empty room but will not in one that is full of furniture.

Animal Echoes

Bats find food by making high-pitched squeaks and then listening for the echoes from insects. Dolphins use echoes to find food, too.

Making Echoes

Good places to experiment with echoes are near high cliffs or under bridges.

If you face a cliff and shout loudly, the sound waves will hit the hard rock and bounce back. You may even hear several echoes if the sound is reflected from different parts of the cliff.

Echoes made under bridges are louder than ones made by a cliff because the sounds have no room to spread out.

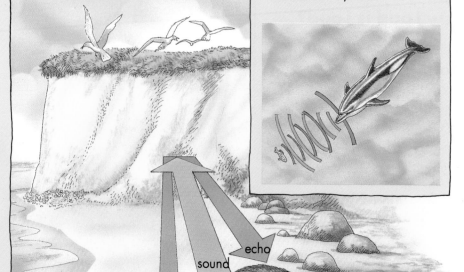

echo

sound

echo

How Do You Hear?

The drawing below shows what the inside of your ear looks like. The part outside your head catches sounds. Inside, there is a small piece of skin stretched tight like the skin on a drum. This is called the eardrum. When sounds enter your ear, they make the eardrum vibrate. The vibrations are amplified and are picked up by nerves. The nerves then send signals about the sound to your brain and you "hear."

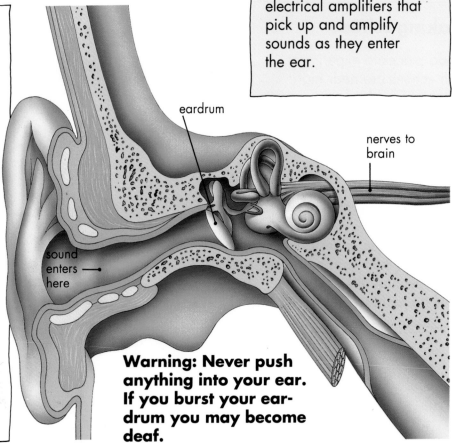

hearing aid

eardrum

nerves to brain

sound enters here

Hearing Aids

Some people can't hear very well because their ears have been damaged. Hearing aids are tiny electrical amplifiers that pick up and amplify sounds as they enter the ear.

How Loud is Loud?

The loudness of a sound is measured in decibels (dB for short). Sounds over 100 dB can damage your ears.
- Airplane 100-150 dB
- Jackhammer 100 dB
- Loud music 90-95dB
- Talking 40-60 dB
- Whispering 20 dB
- Falling leaves 10 dB

earmuffs to protect ears

Warning: Never push anything into your ear. If you burst your eardrum you may become deaf.

Do it yourself

Can you tell which direction sounds are coming from?

1. Put on a blindfold and ask a friend to make a sound, sometimes from behind you and sometimes to the right or left.

2. Try pointing in the direction of the sound each time. You could experiment with different sounds (like humming) and distances.

whistle

point at direction sound is coming from

blindfold

3. Try blocking one ear. Does this make it easier or more difficult to tell the direction of the sound?

👁 Eye-Spy

Watch for animals using their ears. Hares can twist their long ears around so they can check where a sound is coming from. Sometimes you can see birds tilting their heads toward sounds, too.

Light Waves

Without light from the Sun, the Earth would be a dark, cold, lifeless place. Light is a kind of energy. We use light to see. Plants use it to grow.

Like sound, light travels in waves. But light does not need to travel through air or water. It can pass through empty space where there is no air or water to carry it. Light waves travel in straight lines, but they travel so fast we can't see them move. We just see a straight, steady beam of light.

thread

First Light Bulb

The first electric light was invented by Thomas Edison in 1879. He used electricity to heat a piece of burnt thread so it glowed brightly.

Light All Around

We need light to be able to see. During the day, we get light from the Sun. At night, or in a dark room, we use artificial light, such as light from electric light bulbs.

When you read a book by sunlight or by lamplight, the light is reflected from the pages of the book into your eyes. Different things reflect different amounts of light. That is why some things look shiny and bright and others look dull.

Do it yourself

See for yourself how light travels in straight lines. You will need a bright flashlight and some cardboard.

1. Cut out three pieces of cardboard the same size and make a small hole in the center of each of them.

Straight Beams

Sometimes, rays of sunlight are broken up by trees or clouds. You can then see that the light rays are straight.

2. Line up the cards so you can see the light shining through the holes. (You could support them in modeling clay or ask a friend to help.)

3. Now move the middle card from side to side. You will only be able to see the light when the three holes are in a straight line.

look here

Light and Shade

Some things, like glass and water, are transparent. This means that light can pass through them. Other things, like metal and stone, are opaque. They block out the light. As light travels in straight lines it cannot bend around opaque objects, so these things cast shadows. The middle part of a shadow is very dark. It is called the umbra. The lighter edge is called the penumbra.

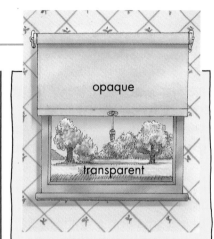

opaque

transparent

Blocking the Sun

Light passes through the transparent glass of the window so we can see through it. But the shade is opaque and blocks out the Sun's light.

Do it yourself

See how shadows work.

Put a piece of white paper on a table under a bright lamp. Hold a small piece of thick cardboard or a coaster in front of the light to make a shadow. Try moving the cardboard toward and away from the light to see the how the shadow's shape changes.

Fly's Eye View

If a fly sat in the middle of the umbra, it would see a dark circle blocking out the light. A fly on the penumbra would see part of the light shining past the cardboard.

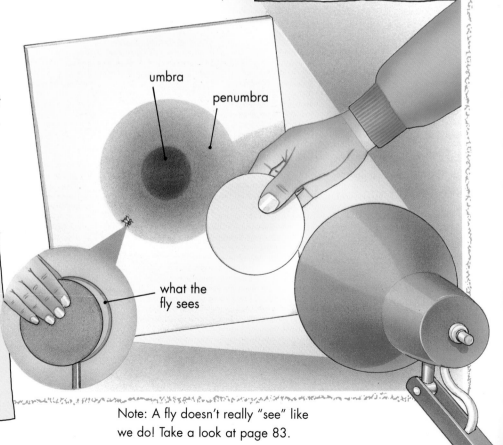

umbra

penumbra

what the fly sees

Note: A fly doesn't really "see" like we do! Take a look at page 83.

Shadows in Space

When the Moon passes between the Sun and the Earth it blocks out the Sun's light and casts a shadow on the Earth. This is called an eclipse of the Sun.

Where the middle of the Moon's shadow (the umbra) falls on Earth there is a total eclipse of the Sun. Where the edge of its shadow falls on Earth there is a partial eclipse of the Sun.

total eclipse—as seen from the umbra

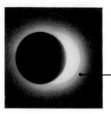
partial eclipse—as seen from the penumbra

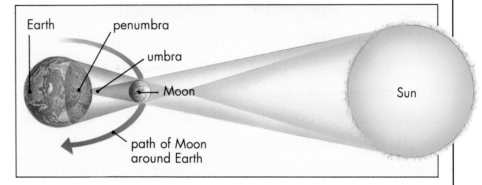

Earth

penumbra

umbra

Moon

Sun

path of Moon around Earth

Do it yourself

Your own body is opaque — that's why you have a shadow. Why not set up a shadow screen and play some shadow games.

Use a good, bright light, such as a slide projector. Hang up a white sheet for your screen. Stand close to the sheet to cast a dark, clear shadow.

Things to Try

- Guess an object from its shadow's shape.
- Draw around shadows made by people's faces to make silhouettes.
- Make shadow puppets and put on a play.

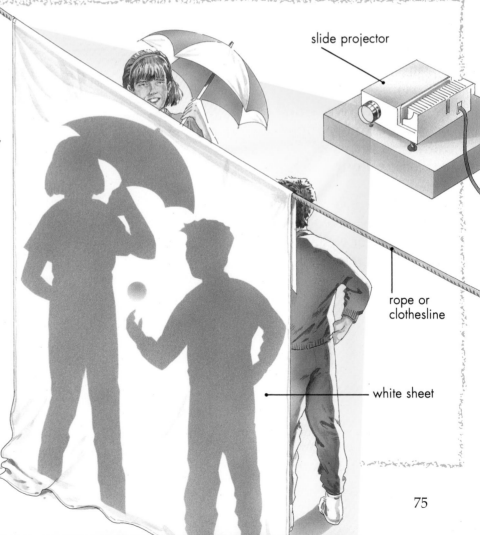

slide projector

rope or clothesline

white sheet

Look in the Mirror

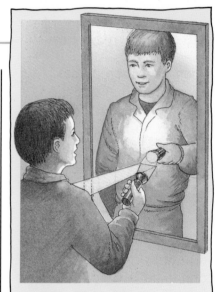

When light hits a surface, the light rays are reflected, or bounced back. Flat, shiny surfaces reflect light best. That's why mirrors are made of flat, highly polished glass with a shiny silver coating on the back. When you look in a mirror you can see a reflection of yourself. Mirrors can be used to change the direction of light to see into awkward spots — like a dentist looking at your back teeth!

👁 Eye-Spy

If you shine a flashlight into a mirror you can see how the mirror reflects the beam of light.

Do it yourself

Find one or two small mirrors and try these different ways of reflecting light.

1. Can you read the numbers? You could practice mirror writing and send secret messages to your friends.

①

2. Catch the Sun's light and send signals.

3. See around corners.

4. Make kaleidoscope patterns. (Place a mirror on each line.)

②

place mirror on blue line

③

④

Note: Never look directly at the Sun, even when it is reflected in a mirror.

76

Do it yourself

Make a periscope to look over the heads of a crowd of people or to peep over a wall.

1. Cut out two holes of the same size at the top and bottom of an empty juice or milk carton. One hole must be on each side.

2. Measure and draw two squares on both sides of each hole and divide the squares with diagonal lines. This is to help you make sure that the mirrors are at the same angle of 45°. Ask an adult to help.

3. Cut out two diagonal slits on each side, as shown. They should be just big enough to slide your mirrors through.

4. Slip the mirrors in place with the reflecting sides facing each other.

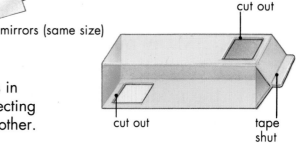

cardboard carton

mirrors (same size)

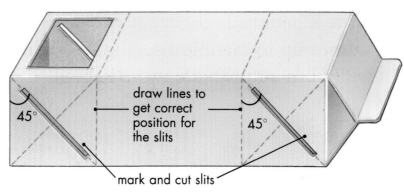

cut out

cut out

tape shut

draw lines to get correct position for the slits

45°

45°

mark and cut slits

The picture below shows how the mirrors change the direction of light. Light hits the top mirror and is reflected down to the bottom mirror and then into your eyes.

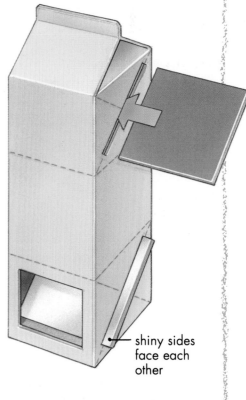

shiny sides face each other

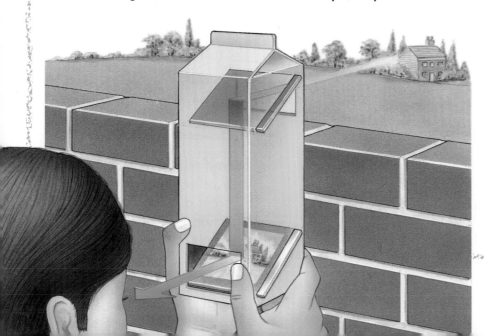

Amazing Mirrors

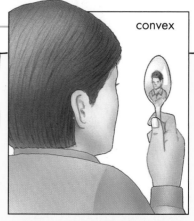

convex

Many mirrors are flat, but some are curved. A concave mirror curves down in the middle. If you stand close to a concave mirror it magnifies you, so you look bigger. If you stand farther away, your reflection will be upside down. A convex mirror curves up in the middle. It makes you look smaller but you can see more behind.

Eye-Spy

Look at your reflection in a bright, shiny spoon. In the convex side, you look smaller but you can see a lot of the room behind you. In the concave side, your image will be big if you hold the spoon close but smaller and upside down if you hold it farther away.

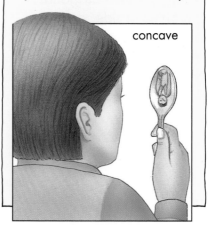

concave

Curved mirrors can be fun! They reflect the light in different directions so your reflection can look stretched, squashed, or twisted.

Bending Light

A straight straw in a glass of water looks bent. This is because light travels more slowly through water than it does through air, and when light slows down it can also change direction. This is called refraction. Glass refracts light, too. Look at some stamps through the bottom of a thick glass and see how their shape changes.

Do it yourself

Test refraction with this magic coin trick. You will need a glass, a coin, a marker, and some water.

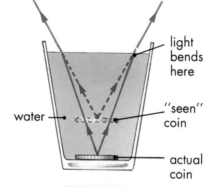

water — "seen" coin
light bends here
actual coin

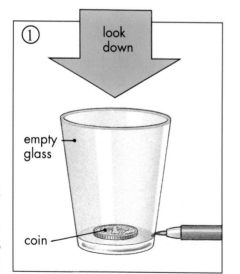

① look down
empty glass
coin

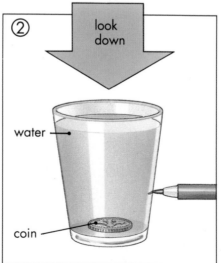

② look down
water
coin

1. Put a coin in the bottom of an empty glass. Look down into the glass and, at the same time, lower the marker along the side until you think it is at the same height as the coin. Were you right?

2. Now fill the glass with water and try the experiment again. You will probably find that you do not lower your marker far enough. This is because refraction makes the water look shallower than it really is.

How Lenses Work

Lenses are pieces of glass or clear plastic that are specially curved to bend light by refraction. If you look through a concave lens, things look smaller. Convex lenses can make things look bigger. Magnifying glasses and microscopes have convex lenses.

The lenses in eyeglasses help people see more clearly. We say that people who wear glasses with concave lenses are near-sighted, and people who wear glasses with convex lenses are farsighted.

👁 Eye-Spy

Do you or your friends wear glasses? Are the glasses concave or convex? The box on the next page tells you how to test them.

Do it yourself

Make a simple magnifier to make things look bigger.

1. Cut a hole in a piece of cardboard or use a slide mount.

2. Cover the hole with clear plastic tape and use a pencil to drip a single drop of water over it. The rounded droplet should magnify things slightly.

You could also try looking at things through the bottom of a thick glass or a glass filled with water.

clear tape

Testing Lenses

Collect some old pairs of glasses. First, look at some print in a book. If the words look smaller, the lenses are concave. If they look bigger, the lenses are convex.

Another test for lenses is to look at the shadows they cast on a sheet of paper. Concave lenses spread the light so they cast a big, dark shadow. Convex lenses concentrate the light. Their shadow is small and bright.

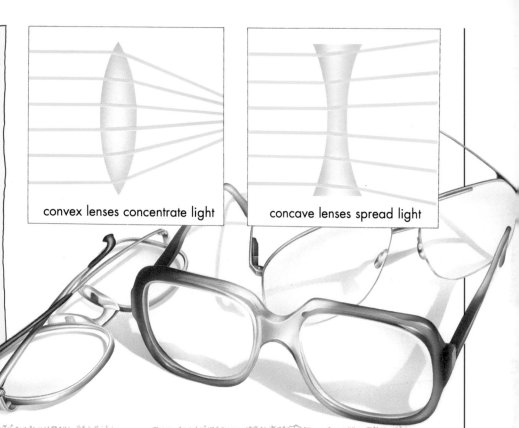

convex lenses concentrate light

concave lenses spread light

Do it yourself

Try this experiment with a convex lens from an old pair of reading glasses or a magnifying glass to see how it concentrates light.

Stand opposite a sunny window and move your lens toward a sheet of white paper until you can see an image of the window and the scene outside. The image will be upside down. The lenses in your eyes work in a similar way. Look at the box at the bottom of the next page.

How Do You See?

Look at your eyes in a mirror. The black spot in the middle is called the pupil. The colored part around the pupil is the iris. The size of the iris changes to make the pupil bigger or smaller. In very bright light the pupil gets smaller so you are not dazzled. In dim light the pupil gets larger to let more light into your eye. If you go into a dark room after being in strong sunlight you can't see much at first. But after a while your eyes adjust and you can see more clearly.

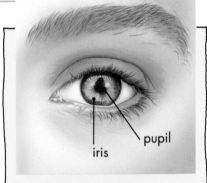

Looking at Eyes

Look at your eyes in a mirror. Close them. Count to 20. Open your eyes. Your pupils will be larger to let in more light.

How Eyes Work

The lens collects the light that enters your eye and focuses a small picture onto the retina at the back of your eye. (This works in a similar way to the lens you used in the activity on page 81.) The retina sends messages about the picture to your brain. The brain sorts out the image so it looks the right way up, and you can make sense of what you see.

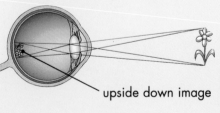

upside down image

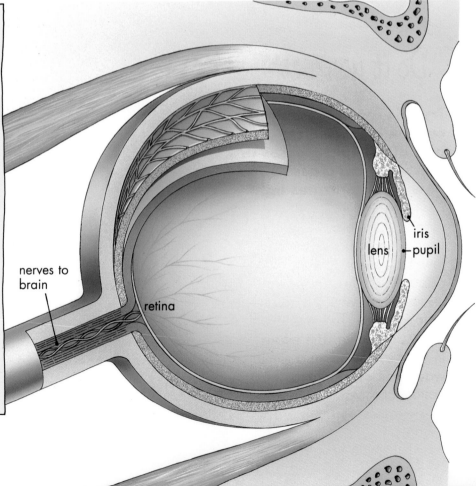

nerves to brain

retina

iris

lens

pupil

Seeing in the Dark

Owls and cats hunt for food at night. Owls have large pupils to collect as much light as possible.

During the day, a cat's pupils are narrow slits, but at night they become wider to let in more light.

day   night

Seeing all Around

A fly has large, dome-shaped eyes. Each eye is made up of thousands of tiny lenses and no two lenses point in the same direction. A fly can therefore see danger coming from most directions — it's almost impossible to sneak up on a fly!

Eye-Spy

Some people are color blind. This means that they cannot tell the difference between different colors.

For example, someone who cannot tell the difference between red and green may not be able to see the correct numbers in the circles on the right. People with normal sight read the top number as 5 and the bottom one as 8. Those with red-green color blindness may read the numbers as 2 and 3. A few people are completely color blind. They see everything in just black, white, and gray.

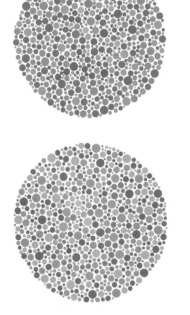

83

Light of Many Colors

Although sunlight looks white, it is really made up of different colors. You can sometimes see these colors when sunlight passes through glass or water. The glass or water bends the colors by different amounts, and this makes them spread out in a rainbow pattern which we call the spectrum.

If it rains when the Sun is shining, the raindrops in the air sometimes separate the colors of sunlight and you see a rainbow in the sky.

Rainbow Colors

A rainbow has all the colors of the spectrum — red, orange, yellow, green, blue, indigo, and violet.

Do it yourself

Here is an easy way to make your own rainbow.

Lay a mirror at an angle in a dish of water. Stand the dish in front of a sunny window so that the light travels into the water and is reflected from the mirror onto some cardboard. The water covering the mirror should split the sunlight into the colors of the spectrum.

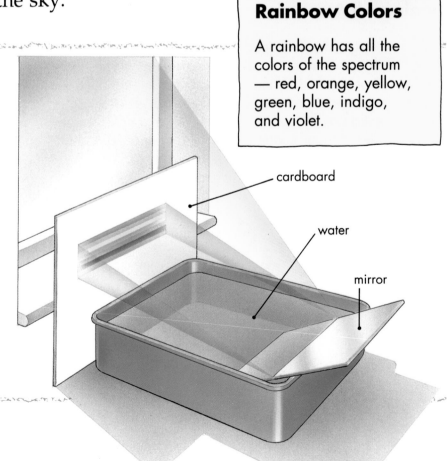

cardboard

water

mirror

SOLIDS AND LIQUIDS

What's It Made Of?

Have you ever wondered what makes one thing different from another? A ball, a drop of water, the wind, are all very different because they are made from different materials.

Most materials are solid, such as metal and wood. Solids don't change shape unless you cut, bend, or break them. Some solids, like glass, break easily. Some, like stone and many plastics, are very strong.

Other materials are liquid. Water is a liquid. It flows and doesn't have a shape of its own.

Solids don't last forever. Glass breaks easily. Cloth and paper rot. Stone wears away, and some metals rust (see page 103).

👁 Eye-Spy

Make a collection of different solids and decide whether they are made of wood, metal, plastic, stone, rubber, glass, or something else.

Here are five solid materials that look and feel different.
1. Metals are strong. They can be sharpened into blades for cutting.

A third kind of material is gas. Air is a gas. You can't see it and it is so thin you can pass your hand through it. Yet you can feel air when it blows over your face and hands.

2. Rubber is light and grips well. It is also springy and returns to its original shape when it is stretched.

3. Glass is transparent (you can see through it), but it breaks if you drop it.

4. Most clothes are woven from fibers (fine threads). Woven fibers are strong and flexible — they bend easily.

5. Plastic is strong, light, and waterproof. It doesn't rot or rust and it can be made into any shape.

Do it yourself

Look more closely at your collection of solids through a magnifying glass.

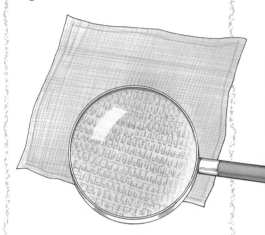

See how cloth is made up of tiny woven threads. Glass, metal, and many plastics look shiny and smooth. Some rocks are made up of differently colored shiny grains.

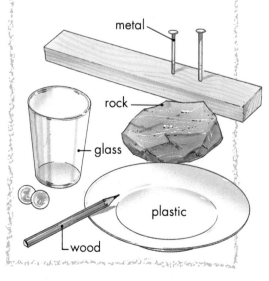

metal

rock

glass

plastic

wood

Materials All Around

Everything we use is made from materials. Some, like cotton, come from plants. Others, like wool, come from animals. Many buildings are made from stone which is cut or dug from the ground. Cotton, wool, and stone are all natural materials.

Some natural materials can be made into other things. Oil can be made into plastics. Coal can be made into paint or soap. Coal and oil are called raw materials. Plastic is a manufactured, or artificial, material.

All plants and animals are made from many different materials. Two of the main ones are water and carbon. (Carbon is the black stuff in the middle of pencils.) In every human body there is enough water to fill 4 buckets and enough carbon to make over 1,000 pencils.

Oil is formed from the remains of ancient plants and animals. We drill for oil and dig for coal under the Earth's surface, through layers of rock.

Wood into Coal

1. Millions of years ago the Earth was covered by thick forests and swamps.
2. Fallen trees were gradually buried by thick layers of mud and sand.
3. The squashed wood slowly turned into coal.

① ② ③

coal

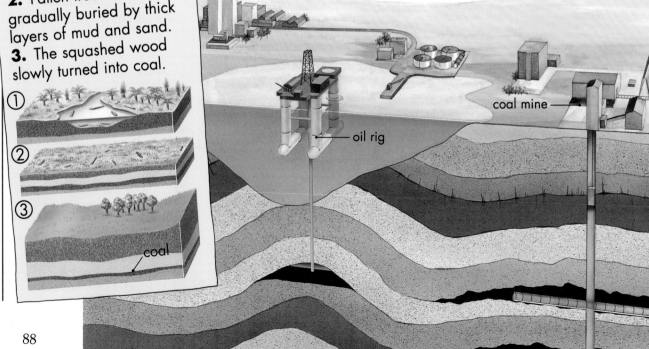

oil rig

coal mine

One of the main gases that makes up air is oxygen. All living things need oxygen. We must breathe oxygen gas to stay alive. Plants "breathe out" lifegiving oxygen.

When materials like coal and oil burn they use oxygen from the air and give out heat (see next page).

What's in Air?

Air is mostly made up of the two gases nitrogen and oxygen. It also contains water in the form of a gas (water vapor) and tiny bits of salt, dust, and dirt.

Do it yourself

See how materials use oxygen when they burn. You'll need a small candle, a saucer, some water, and a glass jar.

1. Ask an adult to stick the candle to the bottom of the saucer with some melted candle wax, and then light the candle for you.

2. Pour about half an inch (1 cm) of water into the bottom of the saucer. Turn a glass jar upside down and carefully lower it over the candle. The glass should just sit in the water. Watch what happens to the candle flame.

watch the candle flame

saucer or jar lid

glass

water level

How It Works

The candle needs oxygen gas to burn. It therefore goes out when it has used up most of the oxygen in the glass. The water rises in the glass to take the space of the used oxygen.

Melting and Mixing

Have you ever sat in front of a roaring log fire? The wood on the fire uses oxygen as it burns. The burning wood gives off heat and turns into ash.

Heat changes materials. It can change solids into liquids and liquids into gases. Heat can make things melt, make them cook, and set them on fire.

👁 Eye-Spy

See how chocolate melts and goes runny on a hot day — it changes from a solid to a liquid.

Do it yourself

Find out how heat affects different materials. You will need three saucers, some ice, a chocolate bar, some butter, and a wax candle.

Arrange a piece of each material around the edges of the saucers (You'll need three pieces of each material.) Put one saucer in the refrigerator, one in a cool room, and one in sunlight or next to a hot fire.

- Which materials melt?

- Which go soft?

- Which stay solid?

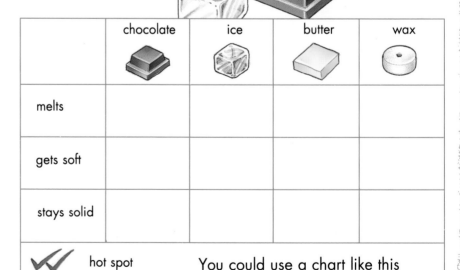

	chocolate	ice	butter	wax
melts				
gets soft				
stays solid				

✔✔ hot spot
✔ cool room
● refrigerator

You could use a chart like this to record your results. Try testing some other materials in the same way.

Do it yourself

See how some liquids will mix together while others don't mix at all, and how some solids dissolve (mix into a liquid).

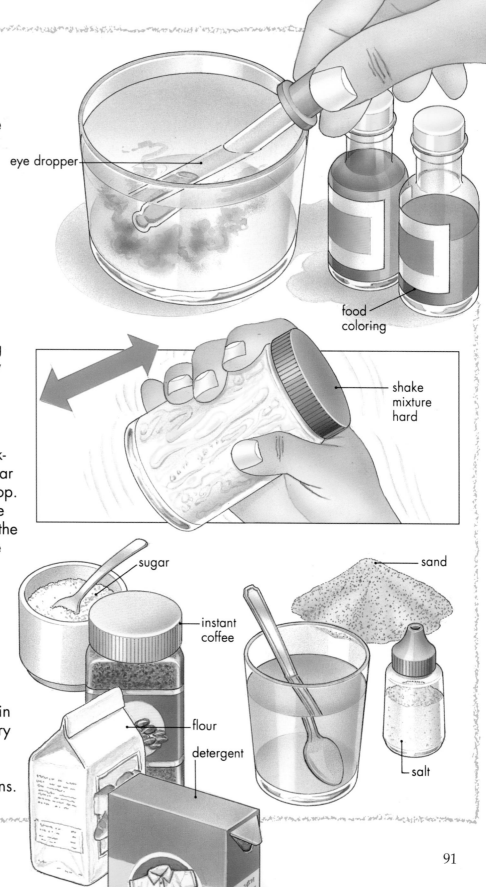

eye dropper

food coloring

shake mixture hard

sugar

instant coffee

sand

flour

detergent

salt

Mixing

Stir some milk into hot coffee to see how the milk and coffee mix to a brown color. Now try dropping a blob of ink or food coloring into some water to see how they mix together.

Unmixing

Pour equal amounts of cooking oil and water into a clear plastic jar with a screw-on top. Screw on the top and shake the jar hard to try and mix the contents together. Leave the bottle to stand and watch how the oil floats on top of the water in a layer.

Dissolving

When you stir sugar into a hot drink it dissolves. Most things dissolve more easily in warm water than in cold. Try stirring the things on the right into hot and then cold water and see what happens.

Mixing Things Together

All solids, liquids, and gases are made up of chemicals. When some chemicals are mixed together they react, or change, and new chemicals are made.

Did you know that cooking is a kind of chemical reaction? When you bake a cake in the oven all the things you put into the mixture react together to make a solid. Beating the cake mixture is important because it mixes in air — it's the air bubbles that make the cake light and fluffy.

Chemistry

Chemistry is the name for the part of science that is all about what things are made of and how they can be changed.

👁 Eye-Spy

Ask an adult to boil some red cabbage and then help you to pour off some of the cabbage water into two dishes. Add lemon juice to one dish and baking powder to the second. See how the chemical reactions make the water change color.

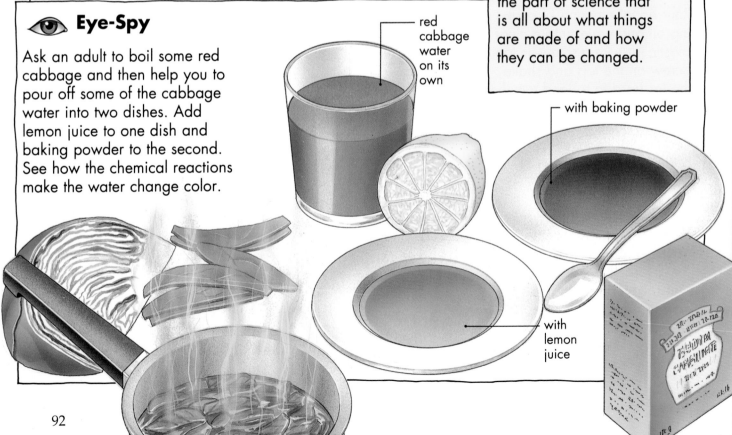

red cabbage water on its own

with baking powder

with lemon juice

Do it yourself

Warning! You must do this experiment outside. It can be very messy!

Make a chemical reaction that will power a rocket. You'll need a small plastic bottle with a screw-on top, a long piece of smooth string, a plastic straw, tape, tissue paper, vinegar, and baking powder.

1. Thread the string through the straw and stretch it out as shown. Pour an inch of vinegar into the bottle and tape the bottle to the straw.

2. Put a few teaspoonfuls of baking powder into some tissue paper and wrap it into a parcel.

3. Gently slide the parcel into the bottle, trying to keep it out of the vinegar until you have screwed on the top of the bottle.

4. Give the bottle a shake and wait for takeoff!

thin string

small plastic bottle

make a small hole in bottle top (ask an adult to help)

vinegar

tissue paper

baking powder

straw

string stretched tightly between two posts

bottle should whizz along the string

small hole

How It Works

When baking powder and vinegar mix together there is a chemical reaction and carbon dioxide gas is made. As more and more gas is made, the pressure builds up inside the bottle, shooting the gas out of the hole and pushing the bottle along the string.

93

Metal Magic

We now use more than fifty kinds of metal and most of them are found in rocks. Some of the more common ones are iron, copper, tin, aluminum, silver, gold, and chromium. As each type of metal has different properties it can be used in different ways. Some metals are better for making cars and others for making coins.

Strong Metal

Steel is very strong. Steel wires and girders are often used to make bridges. Steel is mainly iron with a small amount of carbon mixed in it to make the iron stronger and harder.

copper

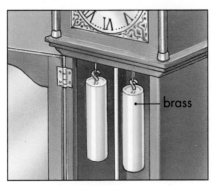

brass

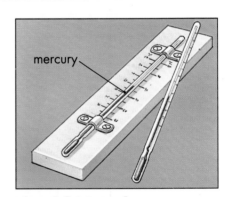

mercury

Flexible Metal

Pure metals (metals that have not been mixed with anything else) are quite soft and bendy. They are used for wires or pipes.

Heavy Metal

Nearly all metals are heavier than water, so they sink. Lead and brass are two of the heaviest metals. They are often used to make weights.

Liquid Metal

All metals melt into thick liquids when they get very hot. Mercury is special. It is the only metal that stays liquid when it is cool.

Do it yourself

Use these four tests to help you decide whether something is made from metal.

1. Does it carry electricity?
Test your material with a battery, a bulb, and two wires. All metal conducts, or carries, electricity. For the test to work, the wires must touch bare metal, not paint.

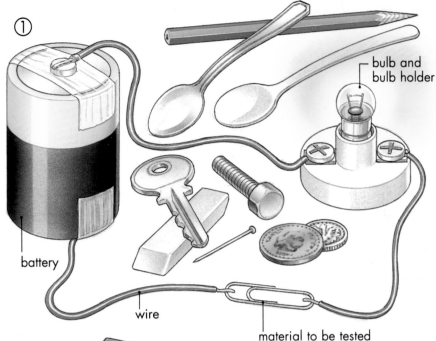

bulb and bulb holder

battery

wire

material to be tested

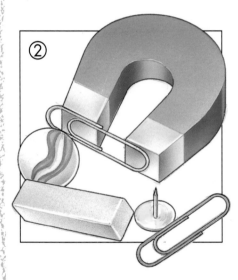

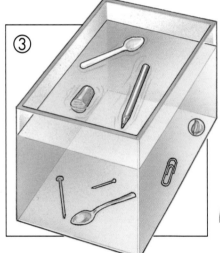

2. Is it magnetic?
If your material is attracted or "pulled" by a magnet, then it contains the metal iron. If not, then it may still be a metal like copper or aluminum (which aren't magnetic).

3. Does it float or sink?
All common metals are heavier than water, so they will sink. Therefore, if your material floats on water it is not a metal and must be made from something else.

4. Can it be polished?
Most metals can be polished to a bright shine. Metals shine in light so they can be used as mirrors. If you can see through your material, then it isn't a metal.

Useful Plastics

Plastics are not natural materials. They're made in factories from the chemicals found in oil. The chemicals are heated in steel tanks which are rather like huge pressure cookers. When the chemicals stick together, new plastic materials are made.

Plastics are lighter and more flexible than metals, but they aren't as strong. Plastics can melt or burn when they are heated. An important property of plastic is that it doesn't conduct electricity, so plastic is wrapped around electric wire to make the wire safer.

Plastic gets soft when it's heated, so it can be made into all sorts of shapes, like these toys.

👁 Eye-Spy

Put a yogurt container in a bowl. Then ask an adult to pour some very hot water over it. Watch how the plastic container softens and changes shape.

boiling water

yogurt container

Plastic canoes and safety helmets don't crack or shatter when they get knocked.

Do it yourself

Make some rubbery plastic at home from milk and vinegar.

1. Ask an adult to warm some creamy milk in a pan. When the milk is simmering, slowly stir in a few teaspoonfuls of vinegar.

wash in cold water

creamy milk

vinegar

2. Keep stirring, but just before the mixture becomes rubbery add some food coloring.

3. Let the plastic cool and wash it under cold running water.

Stretchy, Strong, or Brittle?

Find some different kinds of plastic and try bending and stretching them. Are they stretchy and weak or stretchy and strong? Or are they brittle (do they snap easily)?

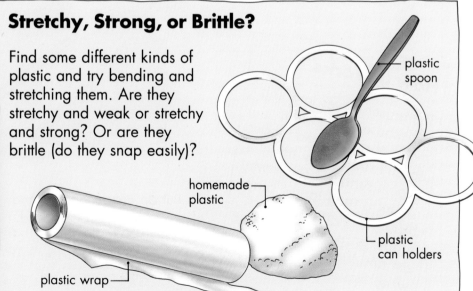

plastic spoon

homemade plastic

plastic can holders

plastic wrap

Springy Rubber

Rubber is made from a white juice, called latex, which comes from rubber trees. At factories, the liquid latex is made into solid rubber by adding an acid—just as you added vinegar (an acid) to the milk in the activity on page **97**. Then the rubber is squeezed, dried, and shaped.

Rubber is a useful material because it is so elastic. It can be stretched and squashed and it will still bounce back into shape.

Collecting Latex

Latex drips slowly into a collecting cup from grooves cut into the bark of a rubber tree. About one cupful of latex is collected each time.

👁 Eye-Spy

See how different types of material slide less easily (make more friction) than others.

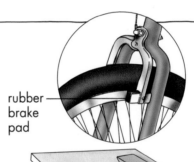

rubber brake pad

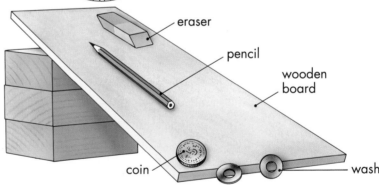

eraser

pencil

wooden board

coin

washer

How It Works

The eraser moves last. This is because erasers are made of rubber and rubber doesn't slide easily on smooth surfaces. That's why rubber is used for the brake blocks on your bike. The rubber grips the metal wheel rim and friction slows the wheel down.

1. Put an eraser on one end of a wooden ruler or board. Then gradually lift the end of the wood until the eraser just starts to slip.

2. Try the same test with a metal coin or washer and a pencil. See how high you have to lift the wood before each material starts to slip.

Do it yourself

Make your own rubber-powered machines.

Spool Tank

Thread a rubber band through the middle of an empty spool. Secure the band at both ends, as shown in drawings 1 and 2.

Wind up the band by turning the longer piece of wood until you cannot turn it any more. Place it on a smooth surface, then let go!

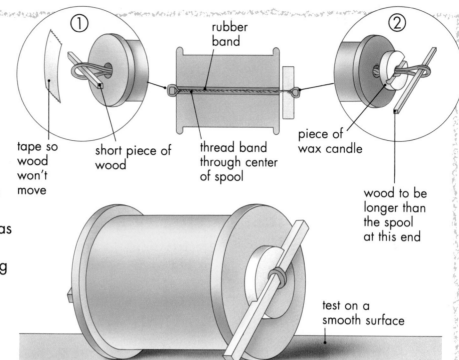

① tape so wood won't move

short piece of wood

rubber band

thread band through center of spool

② piece of wax candle

wood to be longer than the spool at this end

test on a smooth surface

Rubber Roadster

This roadster is also powered by a twisted rubber band. Here, though, the band turns a propeller — like the ones found in modeling kits. The propeller is attached to the rubber band with a hook that runs through the balsa wood and two metal washers. (You should be able to find the washers around your home, or you can buy them quite cheaply from a hardware store.)

Why not hold a competition to design the fastest rubber-powered vehicle!

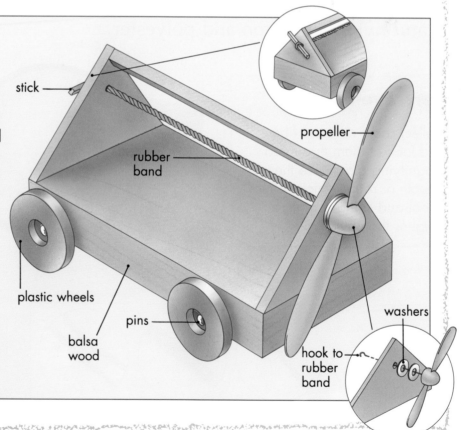

stick

propeller

rubber band

plastic wheels

pins

balsa wood

hook to rubber band

washers

Flexible Fibers

Fibers are simply long, thin, flexible strands or threads. We use both natural fibers, from plants and animals, and artificial fibers, from oil and coal. Cotton comes from the seed pods of the cotton plant and wool comes from sheep. String can be made from plant fibers, and nylon is made from the chemicals in oil.

Plant, animal, and artificial fibers can all be woven to make different kinds of cloth. Look at the labels in your clothes. Some will be made from mixtures of fibers, like cotton and nylon, or cotton and polyester.

A hair is a fiber. Animal fur is just a thick coat of hair. It traps tiny pockets of air between the fibers, keeping in the warmth.

👁 Eye-Spy

Collect some different fibers and look at them through a magnifying glass. Are they smooth or rough, thick or thin? Wool and string are much rougher than nylon.

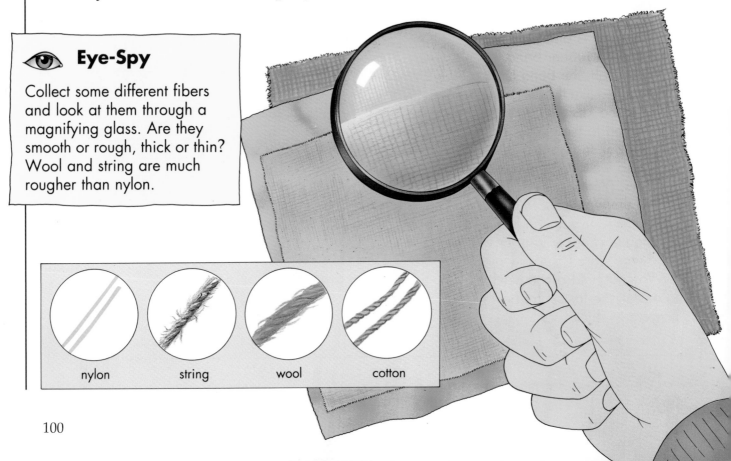

| nylon | string | wool | cotton |

Paper is made from fibers, too. Usually it's made from wood fibers. The wood is separated into fibers by crushing it to a pulp in water. The pulp is then squeezed into thin sheets and dried.

If you look at a piece of cloth and a piece of tissue paper under a magnifying glass you can see the fibers clearly. The fibers in cloth are woven together evenly. But the fibers in paper are just squashed together in a jumble.

secure with rubber band

yogurt container

Making It Waterproof

Cloth is not usually waterproof because of all the tiny holes between the fibers. Try making a piece of cloth waterproof by rubbing it with candle wax to block the holes. See if it has worked by wrapping the cloth around the top of a container filled with water then tipping the container upside down.

Do it yourself

Try weaving a piece of cloth with some yarn.

1. Cut a row of triangular grooves in opposite sides of a piece of thick cardboard.

2. Wind the yarn around the cardboard as shown. This is called the warp.

3. Thread the needle with another strand of wool and weave it in and out of the warp thread. This is the weft.

4. When you've finished, knot the end and cut the threads so that you can remove the cardboard.

stiff cardboard

warp

weft

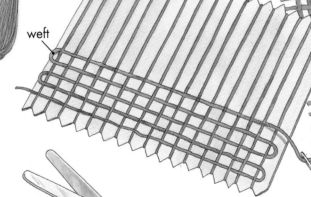

Strong But Brittle

Glass is made from sand — just like the sand on a beach. The sand is heated with limestone and other materials until they melt and mix together. The red-hot mixture is poured into different shapes. It then cools and sets to solid glass.

Glass is a very useful material. As it's transparent, we use it for windows and glasses. It's also waterproof and easy to clean, so it is used to make bottles and jars.

Breaking Glass

Although glass is strong and hard, it is also brittle. This means that it can shatter easily. A glass bottle can carry a heavy weight without breaking, but a sudden knock can make it shatter. Have you ever dropped a glass and seen it break into sharp pieces? (Don't test this out though, you could hurt yourself!)

When broken glass is especially dangerous, a special safety glass is used.

Left: Some glass bowls or ornaments are made by glass blowers. They pick up a blob of soft glass on the end of a hollow tube. Then they blow into the tube and the glass blows up like a balloon.

Rusting and Rotting

Nearly all materials wear out. Most do not last forever. Have you ever left a bike in the rain? Did it go rusty? Iron rusts when it gets damp — it reacts with water and oxygen in the air and eventually bits of the metal crumble to a brown powder.

Wood rots if it gets too damp. Fungus grows on it and the wood loses its strength. Even stone can wear away. It can crack and crumble in frost and rain.

Some types of rock are softer than others. Here, the continuous pounding of waves has gradually worn away the cliffs.

 **Eye-Spy**

Look out for insect holes in old furniture and trees.

Some insects eat wood — woodworms and termites can destroy whole buildings. There is even a bee that makes holes in brick walls. The masonry bee burrows into the mortar between bricks to lay its eggs.

Gold is the only metal that doesn't rust even when it is buried in the ground for thousands of years. Because it stays so bright, gold is called the "noble metal."

Do it yourself

Find out what makes iron rust. You'll need four iron nails, four glass jars (one with a lid), and some nail polish.

① tap water

② boiled water

screw-on top

1. Fill one jar to the brim with water and drop a nail into it.

2. Ask an adult to boil some water for you. Leave the water to cool until it is lukewarm. Pour the water

into another jar, making sure that it is full to the brim. Drop the second nail into the jar and screw on the lid. (Ordinary water has air in it. Boiling the water gets rid of the air and putting a lid on the jar prevents fresh air from getting into the jar.)

3. Paint the third nail all over with nail polish. Drop this nail into a jar of ordinary water. Don't put a lid on the jar.

4. Drop the fourth nail into an empty jar. Again, don't screw on a lid.

Look at the jars every day to see which nails are getting rusty and which aren't.

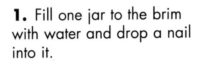

④ empty jar

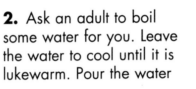

③ tap water

painted nail

nail polish

How It Works

Iron only rusts when both air and water are present. So you will probably find that the nail in the first jar rusts most quickly. The third nail is protected by the nail polish. The nail polish keeps the air and water away from the iron and stops it rusting.

Using It Again

Have you ever counted how many glass bottles, metal cans, or plastic containers are thrown away in your house in a week, or a month? It all adds up to a lot of garbage.

Instead of throwing away glass, metal, and plastic, you can help the environment by using them again. Recyling reduces the amount of garbage we make and saves energy and money.

New From Old

This recycling plant in Germany sorts out different metals. The steel will be reused to make new containers.

Do it yourself

See which things rot away.

Dig a hole and bury a soda can, a glass jar, a plastic container, paper, and some apple slices. Mark the place with a stick. Dig it up after two weeks.

Don't forget to take your garbage away after two weeks is up!

How It Works

Worms and other tiny creatures will have begun to eat the food and paper. These things are biodegradable. The glass, plastic, and metal would just lie in the soil for years.

Save a Tree!

Every year everyone throws away more than 300 pounds of paper. That's two trees' worth of newspapers, tissues, and all the other paper things in the garbage can.

All around the world forests are shrinking. The rain forests are in most danger. Not enough new trees are planted to replace the ones that are being cut down.

- Open envelopes carefully so you can reuse them to send your letters. Buy gummed labels to stick over the old address.

- Buy recycled paper for painting and drawing.

- Save and pack up old papers and comics so that the paper can be recycled.

Planting Trees

In this project in Ecuador, South America, fast-growing eucalyptus trees will be planted to replace trees that have been cut down and burned.

recycled paper

labels

WEATHER AND CLIMATE

Weather on the Move

What's the weather like today? Is it sunny or cloudy, wet or dry, windy or still? In most parts of the world the weather is always changing. Weather changes are blown around the world by winds — movements in the air. Winds are formed when the Sun heats up some parts of the Earth more strongly than others, and the difference in heat makes the air move. Sometimes the weather can be very powerful, bringing violent storms or hurricanes.

Eye-Spy

Where you live, is the weather usually a little different every day? Start keeping a diary to record the changing weather.

When it is raining heavily, it can be unpleasant to go outside, but water is essential to life. Like all other animals, we need water to stay alive.

Scientists try to predict or forecast what the weather will be like the next day or over the next few days. This helps people to plan. For example, you would not want to go for a picnic in the countryside if the weather was going to be rainy and cold.

The weather forecast is very important to many people, particularly to those who work outdoors. For example, farmers need to decide when to plow their land and sow and harvest their crops.

The Atmosphere

Satellite photographs taken from space show a blue haze around the Earth. This is the air or the atmosphere. Weather occurs only in the lowest layer of the atmosphere, nearest Earth. Jet aircraft often fly above the clouds where the air is more still.

Weather Patterns

Although the weather may change every day, each part of the Earth has a usual pattern of weather that is the same over a long period of time. We call an area's usual weather pattern its climate.

Different areas of the Earth tend to have different types of climate — from hot and dry deserts to cold and snowy polar regions. An area's climate depends mainly on how close it is to the equator (an imaginary line around the middle of the Earth), its height, and how far it is from the sea.

City Climates

Cities are usually warmer than the countryside because building stone retains, or keeps in, the Sun's heat.

Do it yourself

Because the Earth's surface is curved, some areas receive more heat and light than others. Try the following experiment to see how this works.

Shine a flashlight onto an upright piece of cardboard. This is how the Sun's rays reach places on the equator, making them very hot. Now hold the card at an angle to see how the Sun's rays are more spread out near the Poles.

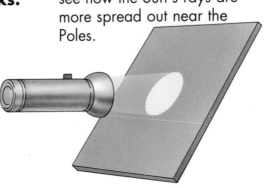

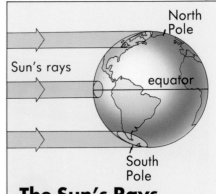

The Sun's Rays

At the Poles, the Sun's rays are more spread out so they have to heat a bigger area. This means the rays have less heating power, so climates are colder.

Polar and Tundra
Cold and dry all year round. Always icy at the Poles.

Cold Forests
Long snowy winters and short warm summers.

Temperate
Not too hot or too cold. Rainfall all year round.

Mountain
Cold and snowy on high peaks, warm on lowlands.

equator

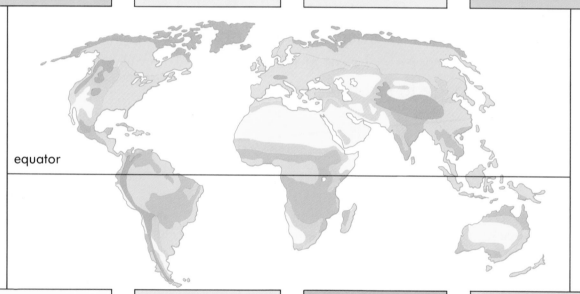

Deserts
Very hot and dry all year, with hardly any rain.

Dry grasslands
Hot dry summers and cold snowy winters.

Tropical grasslands
Hot all year. Wet and dry seasons.

Rain forests
Hot and rainy all year round. Humid or steamy.

Seasons of the Year

In many parts of the world, the climate changes regularly throughout the year. These changes — spring, summer, autumn, and winter — are called seasons. They happen because of the way the Earth is tilted on its axis — an imaginary line between the North and South Poles. As the Earth slowly circles the Sun once every year, different parts of the Earth are closer to the Sun. This affects the amount of light and heat they receive. Look at the diagram on the opposite page to see how this works.

Winter Sleep
Some animals like this dormouse hibernate, or sleep, through the cold winter months. They live off stores of fat in their bodies until the spring.

Do it yourself

Make a model to see how the seasons work. You will need a table tennis ball, a straw, scissors, glue, colored pens, and a table lamp.

1. Cut the straw in half. Glue one half to the top of the ball and the other to the bottom. This is the Earth's axis.

2. Ask an adult to take the shade off a table lamp and switch on the lamp for you.

3. Walk slowly around the lamp, tilting your "Earth" at an angle and keeping it turned toward the Sun. See how the lamp lights up your Earth.

draw the Earth's land and sea areas on the table tennis ball

straw

How Seasons Work

When the North Pole is tilted toward the Sun (1), it is summer in the northern half of the world and winter in the southern half. Six months later, the South Pole leans toward the Sun (3), making it summer in the south and winter in the north.

During spring and autumn (2 and 4), the northern and southern parts of the Earth have more equal shares of the Sun's light. Areas near the equator have no real seasons because they are farthest from the Poles and are not affected by the tilt of the Earth.

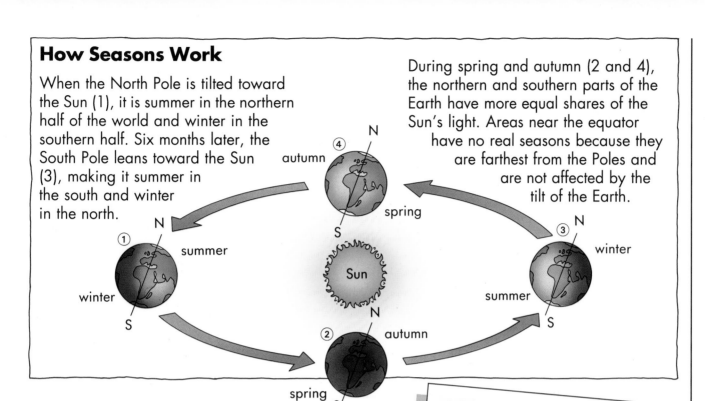

4. The Earth also spins on its axis once every 24 hours, giving us night and day. Try to turn your globe round and round at the same time to see how this works.

turn the globe round and round

day

night

Some tropical countries have a yearly rainy season called the monsoon. It may rain for days at a time and there can be severe floods.

113

Sun Power

Without the power of the Sun, there would be no weather. The Sun heats the land, which passes on some of this warmth to the air. This makes the air move because warm air rises. As the rising warm air moves farther away from the warm land, it cools and sinks. This is how air moves all over the world, causing winds that carry weather changes.

Hot air is lighter than cold air because it is more spread out — the same amount of air covers a bigger area. So hot air usually rises. Try blowing some bubbles over a hot radiator to see them float upward on the rising air.

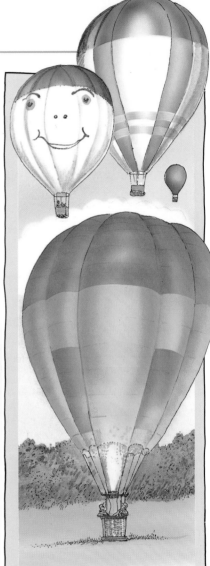

Hot Air Balloons

The air inside a hot air balloon is heated with a gas flame. As the hot air inside is lighter than the cooler air outside, the balloon floats upward. When the air inside cools down it gets heavier, so the balloon starts to sink.

114

Heat and Cold

Changes in the weather are caused by changes in temperature — how hot or cold the air is. So it is important to be able to measure temperature accurately. We can do this with a thermometer. Most thermometers consist of a long thin tube containing a liquid such as mercury or alcohol, which is sensitive to changes in temperature. When the liquids become warm they expand or take up more space, and move up the tube. We then read off the temperature from the scale beside the tube.

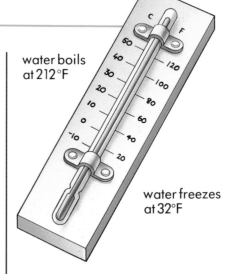

water boils at 212°F

water freezes at 32°F

Temperature is usually measured in degrees Fahrenheit (°F) or Celsius (°C). These temperature scales are based on the point at which water boils and freezes.

Sea Breezes

On a hot day at the beach, there is often a cool breeze — a sea breeze — blowing. This happens because the land heats up more quickly than the sea, warming the air above it. The warm air rises and cool air from the sea blows in to take its place.

At night, the land cools more quickly than the sea, cooling the air above. The cool air blows out to sea, under rising warmer air. This is called a land breeze.

Do it yourself

Make your own simple thermometer using a strong plastic bottle with a screw cap, a thin plastic straw, modeling clay, tape, and thick cardboard. Color the water with poster paint.

1. Ask an adult to drill a hole in the bottle's cap. Assemble the thermometer, making sure that the water comes part way up the straw when you fix on the cap. Leave the water to settle for an hour then mark the water level on the scale.

cold water

hot water

2. Stand the thermometer in a bowl of ice cold water and a bowl of very hot water. See how the water level changes.

Air Temperature

Ask an adult to help you fix a thermometer in a shady, dry place outdoors. Keep a record of the daily temperature for a month.

scale drawn on piece of cardboard

hole through screw cap

modeling clay

plastic straw

116

Air Pressure

When you take off or land in an aircraft, your ears may hurt or feel uncomfortable. This is because your eardrums can feel changes in air pressure as the aircraft moves quickly up and down. But what is air pressure? It is caused by the weight of all the air in the atmosphere pressing down on Earth. Air pressure changes with height and also when air warms up or cools down. Changes in air pressure cause changes in the weather.

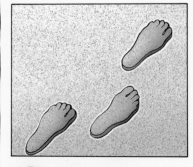

👁 Eye Spy

We do not usually notice air pressure because of the air inside us. This presses outward and cancels out the air pressure that presses all around us from outside. But you can see the effect of pressure from the weight of your body on a beach, when your footsteps sink in wet sand!

At the top of very high mountains, the air pressure is low. This is because the air that surrounds the Earth gets thinner the higher you go.

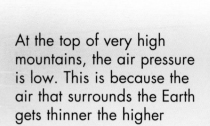

Do it yourself

Try this experiment to see the effect of air pressure.

1. Fill a glass with water up to the brim then place a piece of cardboard over the top.

glass full of water

2. Keep your hand on the card and turn the glass upside down.

flip the glass upside down.

thick cardboard

3. Now take your hand away — the air pressing up against the cardboard stops the water falling out of the glass. Air pressure is very powerful even though we cannot see it.

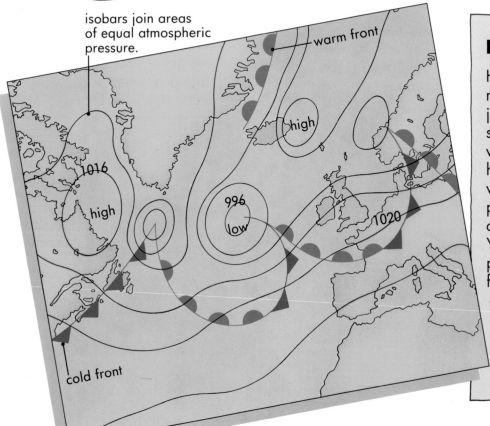

isobars join areas of equal atmospheric pressure.

warm front

high

1016

high

996
low

1020

cold front

Highs and Lows

Here is a simple weather map. Lines called isobars join up places with the same air pressure. Areas with high pressure usually have fine, settled weather while those with low pressure usually have cloudy, rainy weather. You can find out why on pages 122–123. Cold fronts happen when cold air pushes under warm air. Warm fronts happen when warm air slides up over cold air.

Windy Weather

When the wind blows, it is rather like letting air out of a balloon. The air inside the balloon is at high pressure and it rushes out to where the pressure is lower. Winds all over the world are caused by differences in temperature and pressure, and they always blow from high to low pressure areas. Some winds that blow regularly in just one area have a special name, like the cold Mistral wind in southern France. Other winds sweep across the whole Earth.

Thousands of years ago, the Chinese flew kites to frighten their enemies or to measure the power of the wind. Today, we fly kites mainly for fun.

Right: The Beaufort Scale is used to describe wind strength. It has 12 numbers, ranging from calm to a violent storm or hurricane.

1 smoke drifts

2 leaves rustle

3 flags flap

4 paper blows

5 small waves on water

6 umbrellas blow inside out

7 hard to walk

8 9 tiles blown off roofs

10 11 trees uprooted

12 buildings destroyed

Windy Weather

The two most important things about the wind are its strength or speed and the direction in which it is blowing. We use a weather vane or a windsock (a kind of long cloth tube through which the wind is funneled) to see wind direction. Wind strength is measured by the Beaufort Scale, windsocks, or by special scientific instruments called anemometers. These machines have several small cups that spin when caught in the wind. The speed of the spin is then measured against a scale.

The "tower of the winds" was built 2,000 years ago in Athens, Greece. It shows eight gods or spirits dressed to suit different winds.

Gaily colored banners are used at festivals in Japan. These tube-shaped banners flutter and flap in the wind rather like windsocks.

Do it yourself

Make your own weather vane to find out the wind direction.

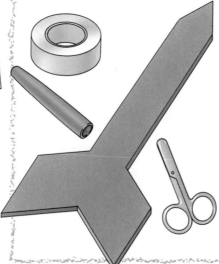

1. Cut out an arrow from thick cardboard and tape a pen top to its middle.

2. Fix a knitting needle or a wooden stick to a heavy base, such as a brick, so that it does not move. Slide the pen top and arrow over it.

3. Put your weather vane outside where it will catch the wind. Remember that the arrow will point in the direction the wind is blowing *from*. Ask an adult to help you check the wind directions with a compass.

Windmills at Work

As the wind pushes the sails of these windmills around, they make electricity. This way of making energy does not pollute, or dirty, the environment.

The fastest sailing ships to carry cargo were called clippers. Clippers depended on powerful global winds called trade winds to carry them from China to the West. The ships used to race each other to break new speed records and be the first to deliver their cargoes.

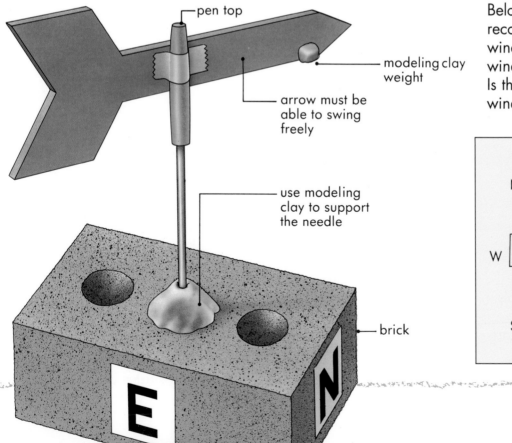

pen top

modeling clay weight

arrow must be able to swing freely

use modeling clay to support the needle

brick

E   N

Below: Make a wind rose to record the direction of the wind. Color a strip when the wind blows from one direction. Is there a main, or prevailing, wind in your area?

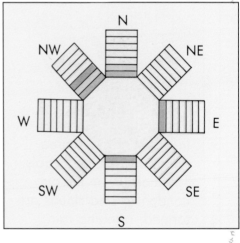

N
NW   NE
W   E
SW   SE
S

Cloudy Skies

Clouds are formed when warm air rises or when warm and cold air meet. Clouds are made up of billions of tiny droplets of water or ice. All air contains some water. Near the ground, this is usually in the form of an invisible gas called water vapor. But when air rises, it cools down. Cool air cannot hold as much water vapor as warm air, so some of the vapor turns into drops of liquid water. This liquid water then collects to form clouds. The process of water turning from a gas into a liquid is called condensation.

👁 Eye-Spy

Steam forms in the same way as clouds, when moist, warm air rises and condenses as it meets cooler air.

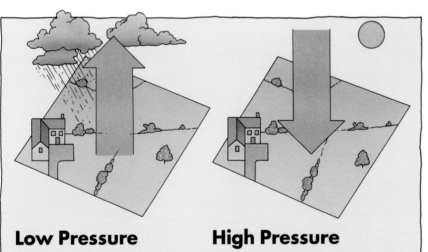

Low Pressure

In a low pressure area, warm air rises and cools. The moisture in the air condenses and clouds are formed, bringing rain.

High Pressure

In a high pressure area, cool air sinks, becoming warmer and drier as it nears the ground. This brings fine, settled weather.

There are three main cloud groups. The highest, called cirrus, are usually made of ice crystals because the air is so cold. White, fluffy piles of clouds are called cumulus, meaning "heap." Sometimes they join together to form huge, towering storm clouds, called cumulonimbus. Flat clouds are called stratus, meaning "layer." Fog is a low-lying stratus cloud.

cirrus

altostratus

cumulus

cumulonimbus

stratus

Cloud Watching

Look at the shape, size, and height of clouds to predict what the weather will be like.

Cumulus clouds usually mean fine weather while cirrus clouds tell us that the weather is about to change.

Rainy Days

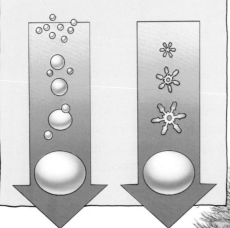

Raindrops form inside clouds as billions of tiny water droplets bump into each other, joining up to form bigger, heavier droplets. Eventually, the droplets become so heavy they cannot float in the air, so they fall out of the clouds as rain.

Every raindrop is made up of about a million cloud droplets. The rain that falls from clouds eventually returns to the air as water vapor. This makes up part of the never-ending cycle that we call the water cycle.

It's Raining Frogs!

Rain clouds sometimes carry other things than water — strong winds have swept up fish and frogs!

How Raindrops Form

Raindrops form inside clouds when tiny water droplets stick together or when ice crystals warm up and melt into droplets.

A rainbow may form when sunlight shines through raindrops — the drops split up the seven colors that make up sunlight.

Ice and Snow

If the air in a cloud is below freezing, or 32°F (0°C), some of the water vapor freezes into ice crystals instead of forming water droplets. These crystals stick together to make snowflakes. The shape of a snowflake depends on the temperature and the amount of water in a cloud. Needle-shaped flakes form in very cold moist air, while star shapes form in warmer air.

When snowflakes are heavy enough, they fall out of the cloud as snow. Sometimes they melt before they reach the ground.

Every snowflake has six points, but each snowflake has a different shape.

Snow acts like a comforter on a bed, trapping tiny pockets of air which keep in heat. Small animals can move around in tunnels under the snow.

Heavy snow can build up behind walls and fences to form deep drifts — even burying cars!

Violent Weather

Violent, stormy weather can be very dangerous, causing great damage and even injuring or killing people and wildlife. As we discover more about the weather, it becomes easier to forecast violent storms and avoid disasters.

Hurricanes and tornadoes form in warm, damp air when winds hurl into each other from opposite directions. Hurricanes grow over oceans, while tornadoes form over land. Hurricanes are sometimes called typhoons or tropical cyclones.

👁 Eye-Spy

If you rub a balloon on your sweater it will stick to the wall because it becomes charged with static electricity — like lightning.

How Far is the Storm?

Thunderstorms happen when warm moist air rises quickly, forming tall dark cumulonimbus clouds. Electric charges build up in the clouds, sparking down to the ground as lightning flashes. The lightning heats the air, making it explode with a crash of thunder. You can work out how many miles away a storm is by counting the seconds between the flash and the thunder then dividing by five. So if you count five seconds, the storm is a mile away.

Right: On this satellite photograph you can see a hurricane's swirling circular clouds that bring torrential rain. In the middle of the storm is a circle where the air is calm and still. This is often called the "eye" of the storm.

Tornado Facts

- Tornadoes or "twisters" are whirling funnels of air that form between the bottom of a storm cloud and the ground.
- Tornadoes last from 15 minutes to 5 hours.
- Some tornadoes can lift heavy objects like trucks right off the ground.
- In the United States, there are about 700 tornadoes every year.
- The word "tornado" comes from *tronada*, the Spanish word for thunderstorm.

Changing the Weather

Our climate has changed many times since Earth was formed millions of years ago. However, the pollution caused by people may be changing the climate much faster than it would change naturally. One of these changes is called the greenhouse effect. This is a warming of the Earth's climate by some gases that act like the glass windows of a greenhouse, trapping heat inside the atmosphere. Greenhouse gases include carbon dioxide, which is produced when fuels like coal, oil, and gas are burned.

Some scientists believe that the dinosaurs died out when the Earth's climate grew cooler and it became too cold for the dinosaurs to survive.

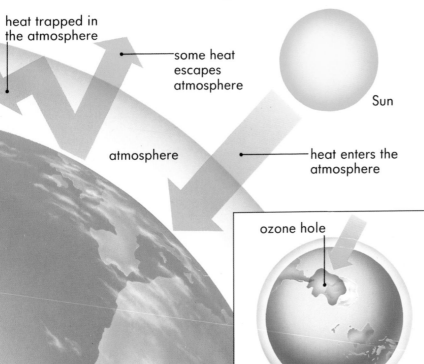

heat trapped in the atmosphere

some heat escapes atmosphere

Sun

atmosphere

heat enters the atmosphere

ozone hole

Ozone Holes

Ozone is a type of gas. It forms a layer in the atmosphere, shielding Earth from the Sun's ultraviolet light rays. These rays give us suntans but too much ultraviolet light can harm our skins.

Over the North and South Poles, the ozone layer has become very thin. It is being damaged by chemicals called CFCs (for chlorofluorocarbons), which are found in plastic packaging and cooling systems in refrigerators.

Do it yourself

Test out the greenhouse effect to see how it works.

Place two thermometers in the sun but cover one with a glass jar. Leave them for an hour then check the temperature of each to see which is higher.

glass jar

Keep a scrapbook of clippings from newspapers and magazines about pollution. Look out for articles on the greenhouse effect, ozone holes, and acid rain. What are the latest theories and developments?

What You Can Do

- Power stations burn coal and oil to make electricity and these fuels give off harmful gases when they are burned. So try to use less electricity by turning off lights when you are not using them.
- Use products that are labeled "ozone-friendly" or "free from CFCs."
- Help to plant trees, as trees use up carbon dioxide, the main greenhouse gas.
- For short journeys, use a bicycle or walk instead of traveling by car.

Left: Acid rain can damage whole forests. It is caused by gases from factories and from car exhaust fumes mixing with water vapor in the air.

Weather Watch

Long ago, many people used "sayings" to help them remember natural signs of changes in the weather. For example, "Red sky at night, shepherd's delight" means fine weather tomorrow. It is doubtful whether these sayings work. But today, we have scientific weather forecasts based on detailed information collected from all over the world. These help weather forecasters to prepare special weather maps and to make more accurate predictions about changes in the weather.

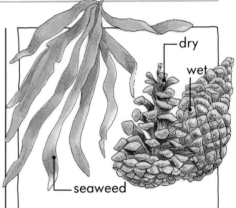

Natural Signs

If rain is on the way, seaweed hung outside will feel damp, and pine cones will close up.

Weather Stations

All over the world, weather stations on land and on ships at sea continually record changing weather conditions. This photograph shows a weather station in Colorado. Balloons like this one are used to measure wind speeds. Some balloons are launched high into the atmosphere to record air pressure and temperature. Information from thousands of weather stations is sent around the world so that different countries can produce their own weather reports.

RIVERS AND OCEANS

Water in our World

Almost three-fourths of the Earth's surface is covered with water, making the planet look blue from space. Water is essential to life on Earth. Without it, all animals and plants would die. Oceans and seas make up most of the world's water. They contain salty water. Water that is not salty — fresh water — comes from rain which fills our ponds, streams, lakes, and rivers. Water is also trapped in glaciers, or rivers of ice, and in huge blocks of ice, called icebergs.

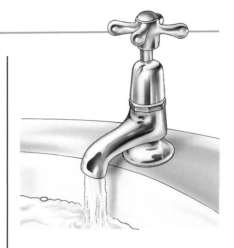

How much water do you use every day? In North America and Europe, each person uses over two bathtubs full. In Asia, people use much less.

👁 Eye-Spy

Do you live near a stream or a river, or even by the ocean? Why not start a scrapbook about it. Paste in photographs or drawings to show its wildlife and how people use the water.

stream

Many rivers start in hills and mountains as small, fast-flowing streams. As the water rushes downhill, it cuts deep valleys through the land.

In the middle part of a river, the water flows more slowly in a wide, flat valley. The river curves from side to side in loops called meanders.

132

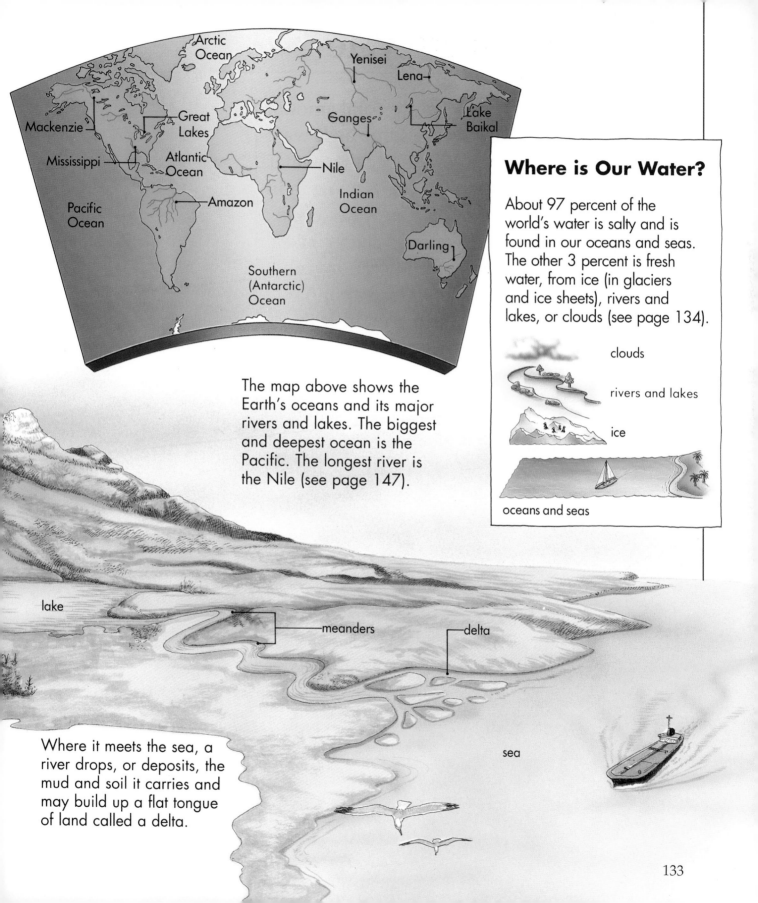

Arctic
Ocean

Yenisei

Lena

Mackenzie

Great
Lakes

Ganges

Lake
Baikal

Mississippi

Atlantic
Ocean

Nile

Pacific
Ocean

Amazon

Indian
Ocean

Darling

Southern
(Antarctic)
Ocean

The map above shows the
Earth's oceans and its major
rivers and lakes. The biggest
and deepest ocean is the
Pacific. The longest river is
the Nile (see page 147).

Where is Our Water?

About 97 percent of the
world's water is salty and is
found in our oceans and seas.
The other 3 percent is fresh
water, from ice (in glaciers
and ice sheets), rivers and
lakes, or clouds (see page 134).

clouds

rivers and lakes

ice

oceans and seas

lake

meanders

delta

sea

Where it meets the sea, a
river drops, or deposits, the
mud and soil it carries and
may build up a flat tongue
of land called a delta.

The Water Cycle

Did you know that the total amount of water on Earth is the same as it was over 4 billion years ago? This is because water rains down from the sky then rises up again in a never-ending journey called the water cycle. The Sun heats the liquid water in rivers, lakes, and oceans, turning some of it into an invisible gas called water vapor. The water vapor evaporates, or disappears, into the air. If the air rises and cools down, the water vapor condenses, or turns back, into droplets of liquid water.

Try marking the edge of a puddle with chalk, string, or a row of pebbles to see how long it takes for the water to evaporate. Do puddles dry up faster in the sunshine or in the shade?

Water All Around

Water falls from clouds as rain or snow (1) and collects in rivers, lakes, seas, and oceans (2). The Sun's heat turns some water into water vapor in the air (3). The air rises and cools and some water vapor turns back into liquid water, forming clouds (4).

Do it yourself

Plants take up water through their roots and give off water through their leaves. If you grow plants in a sealed jar, they will be able to use the same water over and over again, just like the Earth's real water cycle.

3. Put the top on the bottle and leave it in a shady place.

4. See how water given off by the plants condenses on the cool sides of the bottle and runs down into the soil. The plants can use the water again and again.

More Things to Try

Ask an adult to hold a spoon in the jet of steam from a boiling kettle. Watch how water condenses on the cold spoon to form droplets — just like the raindrops falling from clouds.

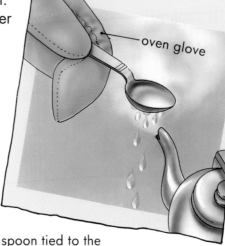

oven glove

spoon tied to the end of a stick

drops of water

1. Place a large plastic bottle on its side and spoon in a layer of gravel with a layer of good soil on top.

2. Use thin sticks to push small plants, such as ivy, ferns, and mosses, into the soil. Press down the soil around the plants with a thread spool tied to a stick.

Water Under the Ground

Some of the water that falls as rain soaks into the ground, slowly trickling down through tiny air spaces in soil or through cracks in rocks. Eventually, the water reaches a layer of rock — called impermeable rock — that will not allow water to pass through it. The rocks just above this impermeable rock layer become soaked with water, forming pockets or reservoirs of water called aquifers. The highest level of water in an aquifer is called the water table.

Eye-Spy

A sponge soaks up water easily because it is full of holes. In a similar way, soils and some rocks contain air spaces which easily fill up with water.

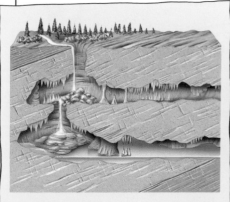

Water easily wears away soft rocks like limestone, forming tunnels and caves. As water drips through cave roofs, it evaporates, leaving behind rocky pillars called stalactites and stalagmites.

stalactite

stalagmite

Desert Oases

In a desert, it hardly ever rains. However, moist areas called oases are found in places where water-filled rocks are near the Earth's surface. The water may have soaked into mountains hundreds of miles away, draining down through the rocks under the desert.

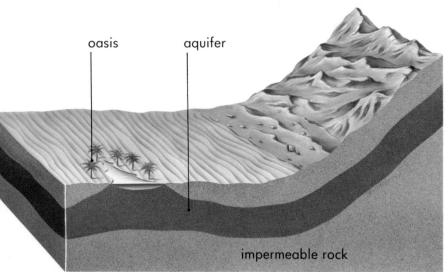

oasis

aquifer

impermeable rock

Do it yourself

Try making your own stalactites and stalagmites. You need two jars, a saucer, yarn, washing soda, and water.

1. Fill the jars with warm water and stir in plenty of washing soda, making sure that all the soda dissolves, or disappears, in the water.

2. Stand the jars in a warm, safe place with the saucer between them.

3. Loop a piece of yarn from one jar to the other so that each end can soak up the water.

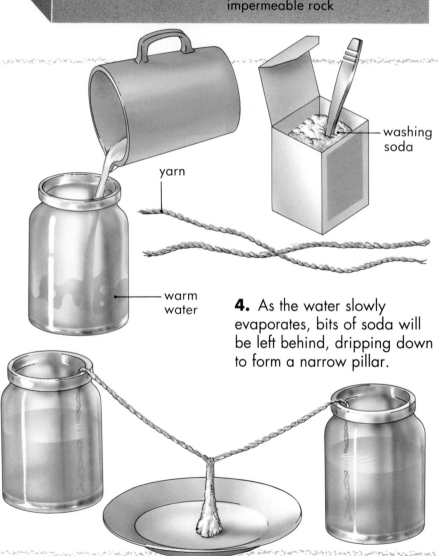

washing soda

yarn

warm water

4. As the water slowly evaporates, bits of soda will be left behind, dripping down to form a narrow pillar.

137

Rivers of Ice

In areas where there is snow all year round, water may be frozen into huge ice sheets or "rivers of ice," called glaciers. Glaciers can be up to 250 miles (400 km) long and are often 1,000 feet (300 m) thick. They form when piles of snow are squashed together to make ice — in the same way that a snowball goes hard when you press it tightly. The ice in a glacier becomes thick and heavy and slides slowly downhill.

The bottom end of a glacier is called its snout. Here it is warmer, so the ice melts to form streams of icy water called meltwater.

Glaciers start high up in mountains or near the North and South Poles where it is very cold. Snow piles up in layers and is squashed and frozen into ice.

As the glacier moves slowly downhill, it grinds and scrapes the land beneath, carrying away rocks and boulders and gouging out a deep, wide valley.

The ice on the surface of a glacier is brittle, like taffy. As the glacier moves, the ice can snap, forming jagged pinnacles and deep cracks called crevasses.

Do it yourself

See how the pieces of rock carried by a glacier scrape against the land beneath, creating a force called friction which slows the glacier down.

Make two blocks of ice as shown on the right. Which "glacier" moves more slowly when you slide it down the slope?

water

gravel and water

Eye-Spy

The pieces of rock carried by a glacier make its sides and bottom rough. Glaciers smooth and polish the rocks they move over in the same way that a rough nail file smooths a broken fingernail.

After the Ice

After glaciers have melted, we can find clues that tell us where they used to be. These include hollows with steep walls (called cirques) and deep U-shaped valleys.

cirque

U-shaped valley

snout

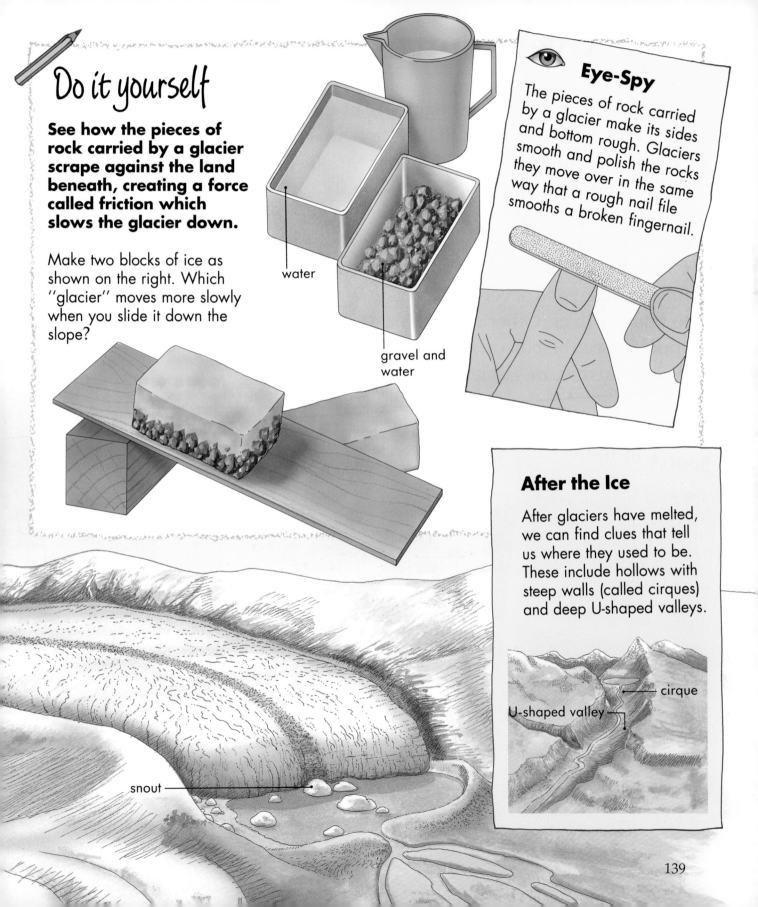

River Sources

The source or beginning of most rivers is rainwater that collects in small hollows or gullies and trickles over the surface of the land. This water does not soak into the soil or the rocks below because the rocks are either already full of water or will not let water pass through them. The trickles of water join up into a stream and several streams flow together to make a river. Other rivers start as mountain springs (see the box on the right) or flow from lakes, marshes, or glaciers.

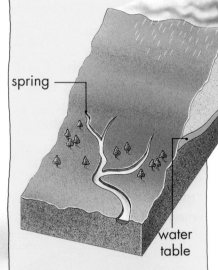

Mountain Springs

Rainwater may collect under the ground, above impermeable rock layers through which it cannot pass. Where these rock layers reach the surface, the water above gushes out as a mountain spring.

Source of the Nile

The world's longest river is the Nile. Its main source is Lake Victoria in Uganda, Africa. The river flows north through Sudan and Egypt to the Mediterranean Sea. See page 147 for more about the Nile River.

Many rivers begin in natural hollows, which fill up with water to form ponds or lakes.

Rivers at Work

Streams and rivers have the power to change the shape of the land. But water on its own is not strong enough to wear land away. It is all the boulders, pebbles, and grains of sand carried along by the water that give a river its cutting force. Sometimes, however, swirling water may split rocks apart by forcing air into cracks in the rock. Some rocks may also be eaten away by chemicals carried in water.

Over millions of years, the Colorado River in Arizona has carved out a huge channel called the Grand Canyon.

Do it yourself

Make your own river and see how it carves out a path downhill.

1. Outside, build a sloping mountain out of damp sand, pebbles, and mud.

2. Slowly pour a steady stream of water over the top of the mountain. Watch carefully to see how the water finds the quickest way down the slope and how much sand and gravel it carries.

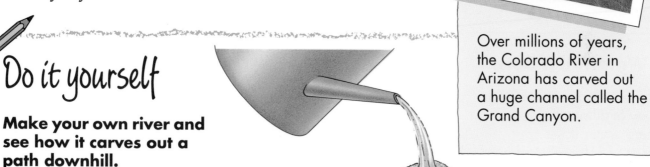

damp sand and gravel

Rushing Rivers

At the start of its course, a river flows quickly, ripping up loose stones and pebbles and hurling them at the sides and bed of the river. After a storm, a river often contains more water, so it is able to pick up and carry huge boulders. With this material, called its load, the river pounds away at the land, cutting downward to form a steep-sided valley shaped like the letter V. This part of a river's course often has waterfalls and rapids — stretches of very fast-flowing water.

A Waterfall is Born

Different kinds of rock wear away at different speeds. So where water flows over bands of soft rock and hard rock (1), the soft rock is worn away first, leaving a step of hard rock (2). Over thousands of years, more soft rock is worn away and the step becomes steeper (3). The water tumbles over the step as a waterfall.

The photograph on the opposite page shows the spectacular waterfalls on the Iguacu River, on the borders of Brazil and Argentina in South America.

①

hard rock

②

③

The drawing below shows the round dips or holes that you can often see in a dry river bed. These potholes are formed when water swirls pebbles round and round, wearing out hollows. The water swirls faster as the hollows get deeper.

pothole

Eye-Spy

Put some gravel in a clear plastic container then hold it under fast-flowing water to see how the water swirls the gravel around.

Winding Rivers

Where the land is less steep, the river begins to flow more slowly, cutting sideways into the land rather than downward. The river now contains more water because other rivers and streams — called tributaries — have joined it, and it carries a greater load. The slower-moving water does not have enough power to carry all its load away, so some of the material drops to the river bed and settles there.

This meandering river looks brown and muddy because of all the sand and soil that it is carrying. A river drops more and more of its load as it slows down.

When a river flows slowly, the water travels around small humps or hillocks rather than rushing over them. This makes the river swing or meander from side to side.

levee

meander

Do it yourself

Work out the speed of a river's current and watch how water flows faster on the outside of a curve.

Push two marker sticks into the river bank, about 300 feet (100 m) apart. Drop a twig into the water by one marker and time how long it takes to reach the other marker.

Watch how your twigs flow around curves. Where do they flow the fastest?

The wide, flat valley floor is called a floodplain. During a flood, the river may break through its banks, leaving behind gravel, sand, and mud, which build up in high banks called levees.

After a lot of rain, when there is more water in a river, the river may cut through the "neck" of a meander. This leaves behind a banana-shaped lake called an oxbow lake.

oxbow lake   floodplain

Floods in China

The Huang He in China has flooded over 1,500 times since people began living there. In 1887, the flood was so bad that over one million people died.

145

Winding Rivers

The point where a river meets the sea is called the river's mouth. Here, the river slows down even further, dropping more and more of its load. Deltas often form at river mouths when the material dropped by the river builds up into fan-shaped banks of new, flat land. The river splits into smaller channels, flowing around the new land to the sea.

 Eye-Spy

Deltas got their name because most of them are triangular in shape, like the Greek letter delta Δ.

 Do it yourself

Do this experiment to see how a river's load sinks faster in salty water than it does in fresh water.

Put the same amount of soil and water in two clear plastic containers but add two or three teaspoonfuls of salt to one of them. Watch how the grains of mud in the salty water stick together and sink to the bottom.

salty water

fresh water

The new land made around a delta is almost flat. So when there is a lot of rain, rivers on deltas often break out of their channels and flood the land. Every year, many people living on the Ganges-Brahmaputra delta in Bangladesh are injured or even killed by heavy floods.

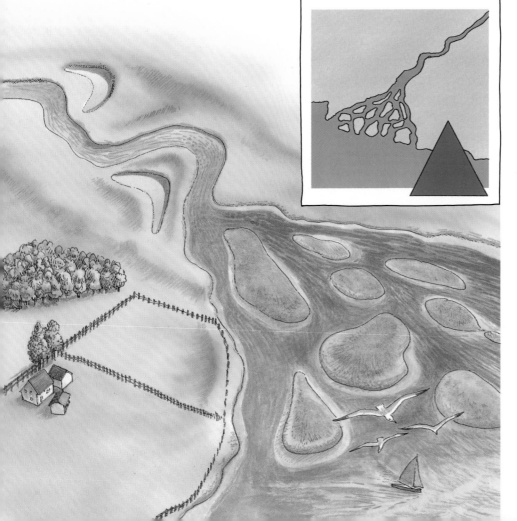

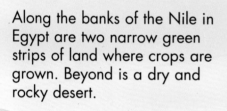

The Nile

The world's longest river, the Nile, is actually made up of two rivers — the White Nile and the Blue Nile. Near the source of the river, at Lake Victoria, there are many rapids and waterfalls. Where the river joins the sea, 4,160 miles (6,695 km) away, there is a vast delta. In August and September, the Nile floods because of heavy rains near its source. The floodwaters used to spread rich soil over the farmers' fields in Egypt, but they are now held back behind the Aswan High Dam.

Farmers rely on the waters of the Nile to keep their crops alive. They use machines like this Archimedes screw to raise water from the river up to their fields.

Along the banks of the Nile in Egypt are two narrow green strips of land where crops are grown. Beyond is a dry and rocky desert.

Aswan High Dam

The Aswan High Dam was built to control floods, provide a regular water supply, and help to make electricity.

Lakes

Lakes are large hollows filled with rainwater, or the water from rivers or streams. They may be formed when glaciers, rivers, the wind, or movements deep inside the Earth create dips or channels in the land. Some lakes are made when water is held back by a barrier, such as the rocks left by glaciers or the hardened rock that once gushed out of volcanoes as liquid lava.

Although some of the world's lakes are huge, no lake lasts forever. They all eventually evaporate, fill with soil and plants or are drained by rivers.

Beavers may create a lake by building a dam of sticks and mud across a river. They then build their home, called a lodge, in the middle of the new lake, where it is safe.

Left: Rivers flowing into the Dead Sea, in the Middle East, carry so much salt from rocks high in the mountains that the lake's water is eight times saltier than sea water. People are able to float easily in such salty water.

Below: On the floor of the Great Rift Valley in East Africa is a chain of long, narrow, and deep lakes, including Lake Victoria, Lake Malawi, Lake Tanganyika, and Lake Nakuru. Lake Nakuru is famous for its thousands of beautiful pink flamingos.

Loch Ness Monster?

Some people believe that the relatives of a huge pre-historic monster live in the deep waters of the Scottish lake, Loch Ness. But no one has been able to prove this by taking a clear photograph.

Six Deepest Lakes

Lake Baikal in northern Asia is the world's deepest and oldest lake. It also contains the most water.

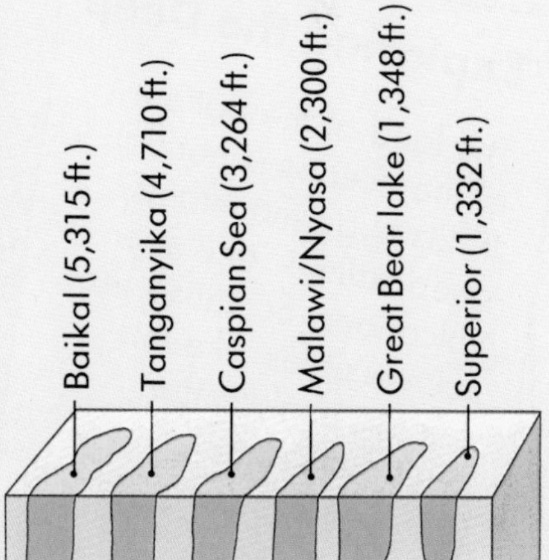

Baikal (5,315 ft.)

Tanganyika (4,710 ft.)

Caspian Sea (3,264 ft.)

Malawi/Nyasa (2,300 ft.)

Great Bear lake (1,348 ft.)

Superior (1,332 ft.)

Oceans and Seas

Most of the world's water is contained in its five oceans – the Arctic, Atlantic, Indian, Pacific, and Southern (or Antarctic). Most of the Arctic Ocean is frozen and covered with ice. During the summer some of the ice melts, releasing huge blocks of drifting ice called pack ice, or smaller chunks called icebergs.

The world's seas are much smaller than the oceans. The seas are usually close to, or surrounded by, the Earth's land.

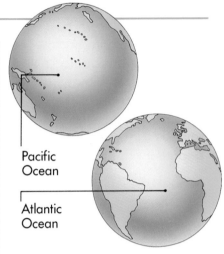

Pacific Ocean

Atlantic Ocean

The Pacific is the world's largest ocean — it is bigger than all the Earth's land put together.

Exploring the Deep

The land at the bottom of the oceans is not flat. It has huge mountains, deep valleys, and even volcanoes. Scientists use submersibles, like this one, to explore the ocean depths.

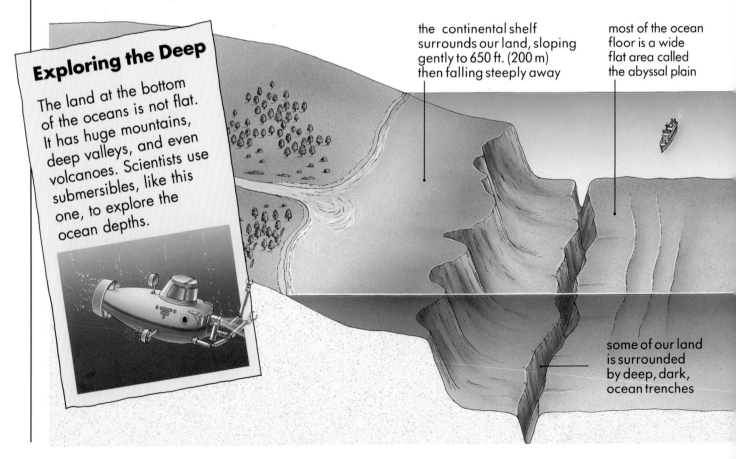

the continental shelf surrounds our land, sloping gently to 650 ft. (200 m) then falling steeply away

most of the ocean floor is a wide flat area called the abyssal plain

some of our land is surrounded by deep, dark, ocean trenches

Do it yourself

Make your own floating iceberg. All you need is a balloon, a bucket or a bowl — and some water!

Follow the stages shown in the drawings. (Ask an adult to help you stretch the neck of the balloon over a cold faucet and knot the end when it is full of water.) See how much of your iceberg floats below the water's surface.

fill the balloon with water

cut the balloon away with scissors after the water has been frozen

the hidden part of an iceberg can be dangerous to ships

mountain ranges called mid-oceanic ridges run along parts of the ocean floor

some mountains break the ocean's surface to form island chains

Deep Sea Fishes

The Sun's light and heat cannot reach deep down in the oceans, so it is dark and cold there. Many deep sea fishes, like this angler fish, produce their own light to help them find food.

Waves, Currents, and Tides

The water in our seas and oceans is always moving, even when it looks calm and still. Winds blowing across the water make ripples, or waves, on the sea's surface, and create sweeping ocean currents. The level of the sea also rises and falls every day in a regular pattern of high and low tides. Tides are caused mainly by the pull of the Moon as it circles the Earth. Sometimes, huge waves called tsunamis are set off by underwater earthquakes and volcanoes.

A wave's size depends on the speed of the wind, and how long and how far the wind has been blowing.

How Waves Work

In the open sea, waves look like they are traveling forward, but the water in each wave stays in almost the same place, moving around in circles. Near the shore, some of the water catches on the seabed. This slows the wave down and the top of the wave curves over and breaks.

Eye-Spy

To see how waves work, try making some small waves in a bathtub and watch a bath toy, like a duck, bob up and down on a wave rather than moving forward.

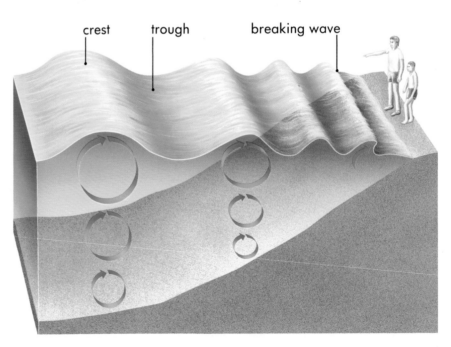

crest   trough   breaking wave

Ocean Currents

Ocean currents are like giant rivers, flowing slowly across the oceans and seas. There are nearly 40 main currents in the world's oceans. Warm currents, shown on this map in red, flow near the water's surface. They are created by winds. Cold currents, shown in green, are created when cold water sinks and spreads. They move deep down in the ocean depths.

At high tide, the sea rises up the shore, dumping seaweed, shells, feathers, wood, and other objects in a ragged line called the strandline.

Most coasts have two high tides and two low tides every 24 hours.

Waves at Work

Waves carry with them the energy and power of the wind. Strong waves hurl rocks and pebbles against the coasts, wearing away cliffs. Breaking waves pound against rocks, squashing air into rock cracks. Then, when the waves pull back, the squashed air explodes out, weakening the rock and eventually breaking it apart. Cliff bases become worn away by the pounding waves until the upper parts overhang. This weakens the cliffs until large sections of rock may crumble into the sea.

Soft rocks, like chalk or limestone, wear away quickly. Houses built on soft cliffs may fall into the sea as the rocks beneath are cut away.

Shaping the Coast

Soft rock is worn away to make bays, while hard rock juts out as headlands. Waves may punch a hole called a blowhole through the roof of a cave. Or caves on opposite sides of a headland may meet to form an arch. If the roof of an arch falls in, it leaves a column of rock called a stack.

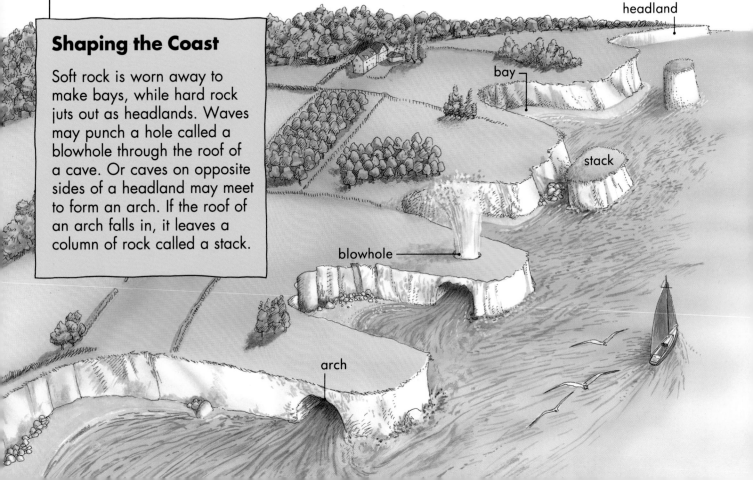

headland

bay

stack

blowhole

arch

Sand, pebbles, and grains of rock and soil are washed onto our coasts by waves or dropped into the sea at river mouths. In sheltered areas, this material builds up to form beaches. On some beaches, the wind blows sand into small hills, or dunes. On headlands, sand may build up into a narrow ridge called a spit. The wind and waves can easily blow or wash away fine sand. To stop our coasts wearing away, people plant grasses, like marram grasses, or build fences, called groins.

Marram grass grows quickly on sand dunes. Its roots bind the sand together and stop it from drifting away.

Building a Spit

Where a coasts curves, waves may carry sand and pebbles on in a straight line, building a long ridge, or a spit.

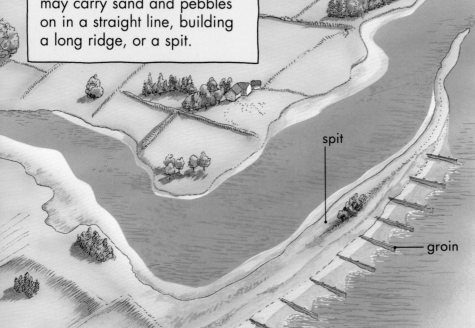

spit

groin

Longshore Drift

If waves hit a beach at an angle, they move the sand along in a zigzag path called longshore drift.

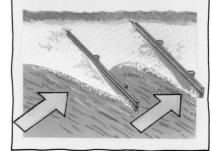

Water Pollution

The Earth's water is much more polluted, or dirtier, than it used to be. Sewage, chemicals used on crops, and waste from factories are washed into rivers, lakes, and the oceans. And leaks and spills from oil tankers add to this pollution. Fishes and other creatures find it difficult to survive in polluted waters and this upsets the balance of life on Earth.

Pollution of the air, or atmosphere, may be heating the whole world. This could make the ice sheets at the poles melt, causing sea levels to rise and seawater to flood the land.

Oil Damage

Oil sticks birds' feathers together so they cannot fly or swim — the birds will die unless their feathers can be cleaned.

This drawing shows some of the main causes of water pollution. We must stop polluting our rivers and oceans to avoid damaging people and wildlife all over the world.

garbage site

power station

farming

sewage plant

factory

mining

oil spillage from ships

Do it yourself

Make a water filter to clean up some dirty water.

1. Make some muddy water by mixing soil, sand, leaves, and twigs in an old container and pouring the mixture through a sieve.

2. Cut the bottom off a large plastic bottle and wedge some cotton batting in its neck.

3. Turn the bottle upside down and support it in a jar. Add a layer of gravel and sand over the cotton, then a sheet of blotting paper. These layers trap the dirt.

4. Pour the muddy water through the filter — but do not drink it. The filtered water is still very dirty!

soil, sand, leaves, and twigs

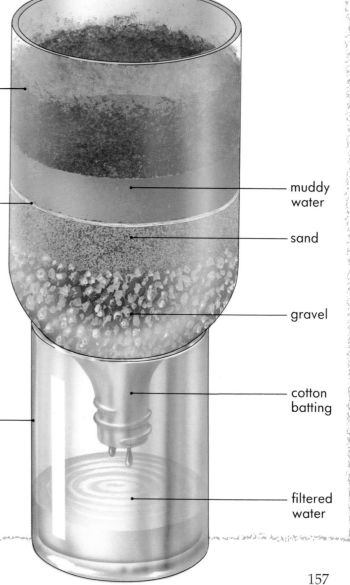

scum on side of bottle

blotting paper

muddy water

sand

gravel

cotton batting

glass to collect water

filtered water

Eye-Spy

Make a record of any water pollution near your home. Look out for garbage by river banks or shores and for oil or factory wastes floating on the water.

157

Amazing Rivers and Oceans

Although we know much more about the power of our rivers and oceans than people living long ago, the world under the sea is still a mysterious and dangerous place.

Do it yourself

Why not start a fact file about rivers and oceans?

Divide your file into sections and use a ring binder so that you can add new pages to each section as you discover and learn more.

Collect postcards, stamps, and photographs and cut out pictures from magazines.

Scientists are still making exciting discoveries about the world under the sea, so look out for newspaper articles about new developments or undersea expeditions.

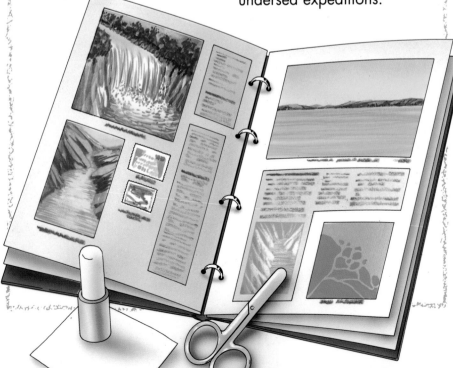

Record Breakers

- Largest ocean — Pacific (64,100,000 sq. miles)
- Smallest ocean — Arctic (4,700,000 sq. miles)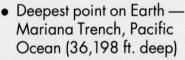
- Deepest point on Earth — Mariana Trench, Pacific Ocean (36,198 ft. deep)
- Highest waterfall — Angel Falls, South America (3,212 ft.)
- Longest river — Nile (4,160 miles)
- Largest saltwater lake — Caspian Sea (143,244 sq. miles)
- Largest freshwater lake — Lake Superior, North America (31,700 sq. miles)
- Deepest lake — Lake Baikal, northern Asia (5,315 ft.)
- Highest sea wave ever recorded (111 ft. high)
- Longest glacier — Lambert-Fisher Ice Passage, Antarctica (250 miles long)
- Largest delta — Ganges-Brahmaputra (29,000 sq. miles)

Maps and Mapping

A Bird's Eye View

Have you ever used a map? Maps can help us find our way to a place even if we have never been there before. Most maps are flat drawings of a piece of the Earth's surface seen from above – the sort of view that birds have when they fly overhead. A map is easier to use than written instructions because it is a simple picture showing where things are. Ancient maps were drawn on animal skins or cloth, and the word "map" comes from the Latin word *mappa*, meaning cloth.

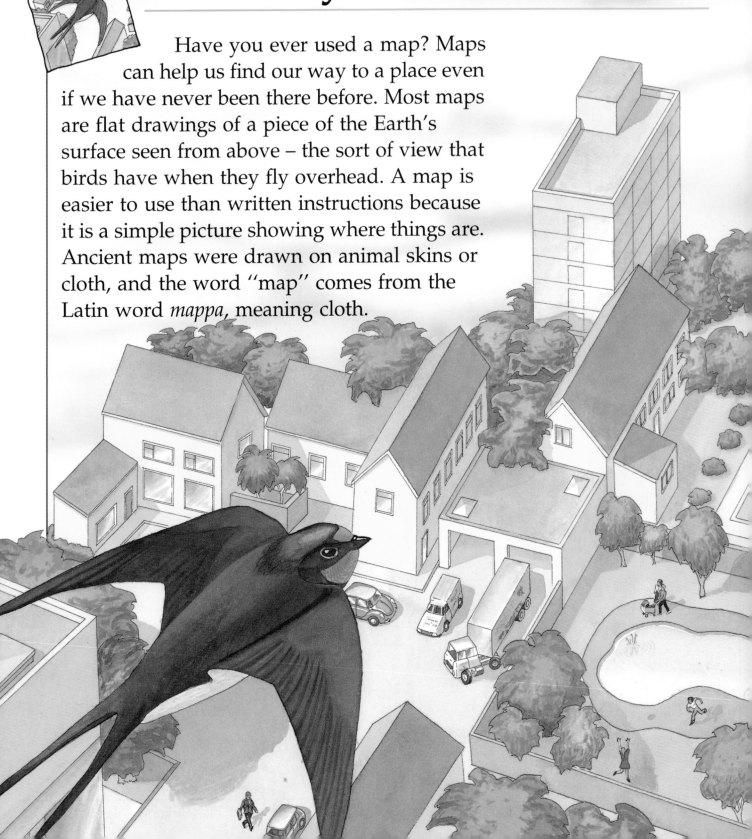

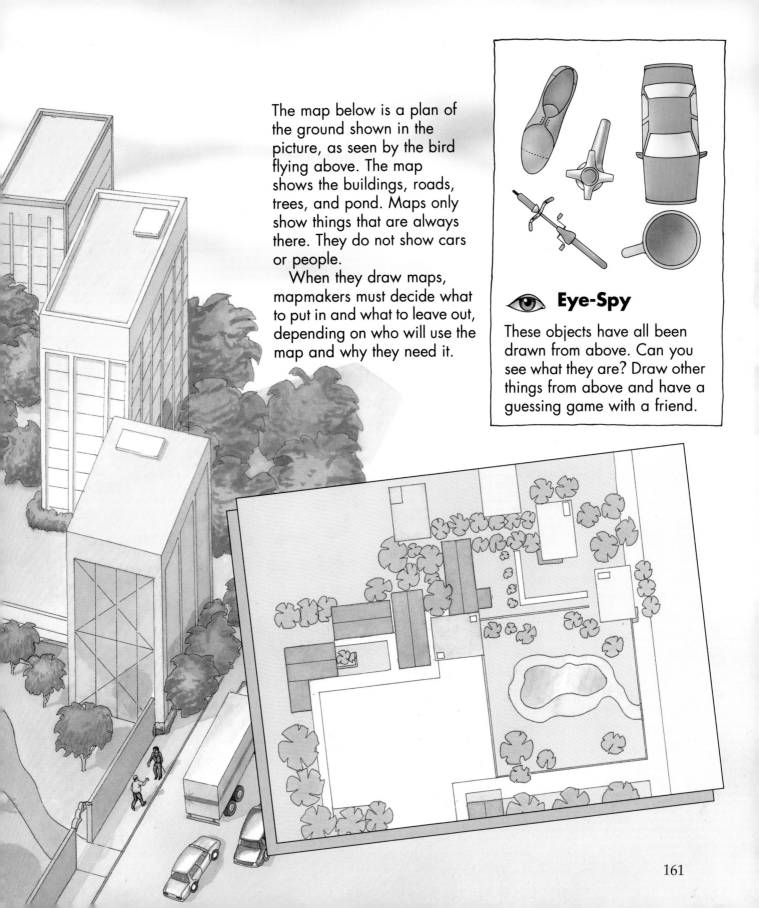

The map below is a plan of the ground shown in the picture, as seen by the bird flying above. The map shows the buildings, roads, trees, and pond. Maps only show things that are always there. They do not show cars or people.

When they draw maps, mapmakers must decide what to put in and what to leave out, depending on who will use the map and why they need it.

👁 Eye-Spy

These objects have all been drawn from above. Can you see what they are? Draw other things from above and have a guessing game with a friend.

Mapping Your Room

The best way to understand how maps work and how useful they can be is to draw one yourself. Choose a small area to start with, like your bedroom. Before you start, decide how big you want your map to be. You will not have room to include everything on your map, just the most important things like your furniture and the door and window. The first thing to do is to find out the exact size of your room and the position of the things in it. The project on the opposite page will show you how to do this.

You will often see large maps like this one in parks. They usually have an arrow or a circle to show you exactly where you are.

My House to Yours

Has anyone ever asked you how to get from one place to another?

Close your eyes and imagine the route you usually take from your house to your friend's house, or try to describe the route shown on this map. Could you give directions so that a stranger could follow them? It's not as easy as it sounds! You need to remember all the important landmarks, like churches or certain stores, and you must say exactly when to turn right or left.

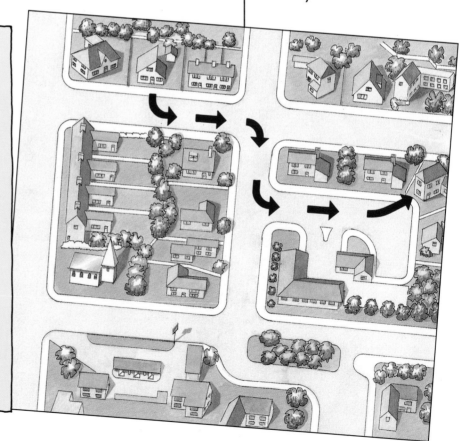

Do it yourself

To make an accurate map of your room, you need some large-squared graph paper, a ruler, and a sharp pencil.

More Things to Try

Make another plan to show your furniture in new places. This is a good way of testing whether your bed will fit somewhere else without moving it around! Try making a plan of another room in your house.

Bed

Bedside cupboard

Window

Chest of drawers

Desk

Door

Chair

21 squares

16 squares

1. Measure the size of your room in footsteps. Count how many footsteps it is across the length and width of your room.

Remember to take small steps so that the heel of one foot touches the toe of the other. In this way, all your steps will be the same size so your measurements will be more accurate.

2. Imagine that one of your footsteps is equal to one square on the graph paper, then draw in the edges of your room. For example, if your room is 21 steps long and 16 steps wide, draw a box on your paper that is 21 squares long and 16 squares wide.

3. Mark in the position of your door and window. Now measure around your large pieces of furniture in footsteps. Then, using your ruler, draw them in the correct position on your plan.

Map Scales

On most maps, everything is shrunk, or scaled down, by the same amount. So on the map of your room, one footstep equaled one square on your paper. You could also have made up a scale in which one foot of your room was equal to half an inch on your map. Map scales compare the size of the map with the real size of a place. Maps can be drawn to any scale. Look at the four maps below. Each shows Florence, a city in Italy, but each map is at a different scale.

These toy cars are 25 times smaller than real cars. In a similar way, maps are drawn to a much smaller scale than the real places they show.

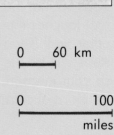

ITALY

ITALY

On this scale of map, 1 inch equals 600 miles. There are about 38,000,000 inches in 600 miles, so the scale is written as 1:38,000,000.

0   375 km*

0   600
                miles

This scale of map shows where Florence is in Italy. As 1 inch on the map equals 100 miles on the ground, the scale is 1:6,300,000.

0   60 km

0   100
                miles

* Some countries measure in centimeters and kilometers while others use inches and miles.
The top scale shows the number of kilometers represented by 1 centimeter on the map.

Railroad Maps

Some maps are not drawn to scale. Instead they are distorted, or changed, to make them easier to understand. For example, on this map of the railroad system in Tokyo, the tracks are drawn as straight lines with plenty of space between the stations. In real life, the lines crisscross the city like a maze so an accurate map would be too confusing.

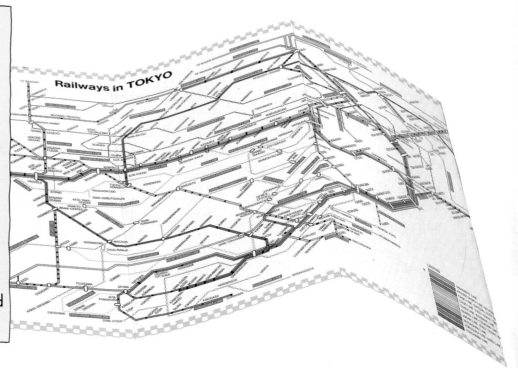

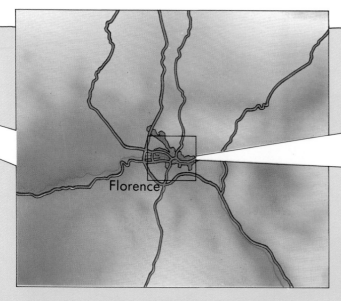

This is a more detailed map that shows only Florence with its roads and rivers. Here, 1 inch equals 16 miles, so the scale is 1:1,000,000.

0 ____ 10 km

0 ____ 16 miles

This is the most detailed map of Florence. It shows just part of the city. Here, 1 inch equals 1.6 miles so the scale is written as 1:100,000.

0 ____ 1 km

0 ____ 1.6 miles

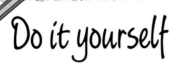

Do it yourself

To understand how scale works, try drawing a "map" of this book.

1. Draw around the book on a large sheet of paper and measure the outline. The book measures 9.5 inches by 8.5 inches.

2. This scale is life-sized, or 1:1, because 1 inch on your paper is the same as 1 inch measured around the book. It can be written on a scale bar (in inches or in cm), like this:

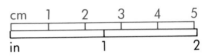

3. The darker blue paper is half the size of the first sheet. Can you draw an outline of your book at half its real size? The scale of your new "map" will be 1:2. It could be written on a scale bar like this:

book

half size

full size

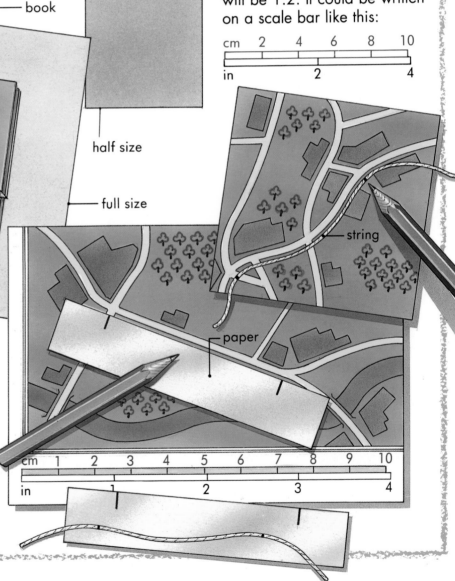

string

paper

To work out real distances from a map, measure the distance between two points on the map. You can use a ruler, the edge of a piece of paper, or, if the line is curved, a piece of string. If the scale of the map is 1 inch to 1 mile and the distance between the two points is 5 inches, then the real distance is 5 miles.

Symbols and Colors

Mapmakers use symbols or signs on maps so that they can give plenty of information in a small space. On the map below, for example, the pictures clearly show where there are mountains and forests. Most maps have a list called a key or a legend to tell you what the different symbols mean. There are no rules about how colors must be used on maps, but mapmakers usually use the same colors for the same things. Water is mostly blue, for example, and forests are green.

Do it yourself

tree

parking lot

freeway

telephone

road

building

water

railroad

fields

lake

Try making up your own map symbols. They should be simple and remind us of the features they stand for.

United Kingdom

M1 or A6(M)   motorway

m   ancient monument or historic building

Λ   campsite

France

autoroute

•Mon!   monument   ⬦ ruin

(o)   campsite

United States

80   interstate highway

state monument, memorial, or historic site

state park with campsite

The symbols shown here are from real maps. They vary slightly in different countries.

167

Heights and Slopes

Mapmakers use colors and lines to show the height of the land and how steeply it rises and falls. Heights and depths on a map are measured above and below the average level of the sea. For example, when we say that Mount Everest – the world's tallest mountain – is 29,028 feet (8,848 meters) high, we mean that its height measures 29,028 feet above sea level.

👁 Eye-Spy

In stores, clothes are often color-coded to help us find our size quickly.

Colors for Height

These drawings show how the hills and valleys that we see in the countryside can be simplified into flat maps. First, an area is divided into sections or bands of different heights.

All land areas of the same height are given one color. The lowest land is usually colored yellow or green and higher land is shown in different shades of brown.

On the flat map below, it is easy to see which areas of land are higher. For example, the highest land is shown in dark brown.

Another way that we can show height on a map is by using contour lines. You can read about them on pages 170–171.

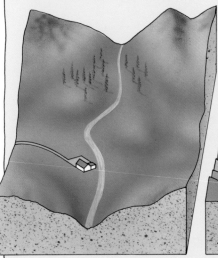

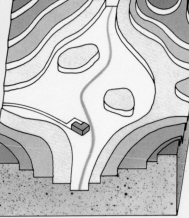

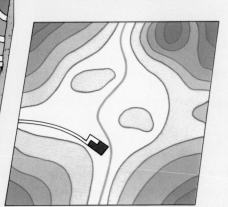

Maps that show the height of the land and other features, like rivers, are called physical or relief maps. They are often used by people who enjoy walking in the countryside.

Undersea Maps

Maps are made of the hills and valleys at the bottom of the sea, too.

Ships use sonar instruments to send sound waves down to the seabed. The time taken for the sound waves to bounce back to the ship is then measured. We know how long sound takes to travel a certain distance, so it is possible to work out the depth of the water.

On sea charts, dark blue is used for deep water and light blue for shallow water.

Contour Lines

Imaginary lines called contours are an important way of showing the rise and fall of the land on a map. Contour lines show all the places that are the same height above sea level. Contours also tell us about the slope of the land. On a steep slope, the lines are close together. On a more gentle slope, they are farther apart. If there are no contour lines, the land is almost flat.

Walkers study the contour lines on maps to find out whether hills will be easy or difficult to climb.

High Hills, Flat Maps

Here you can see how the two hills shown on the right have been mapped using contour lines.

Again, the land has been divided into colored bands according to height, but this time each band has been given a height in feet.

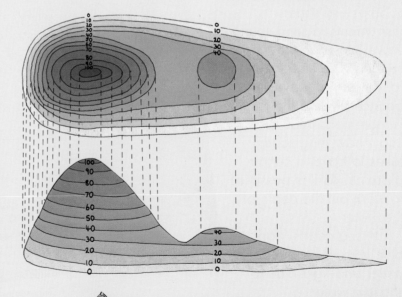

Do it yourself

Make your own contour lines to see how they work. You will need some sand or soil, a wooden board, a pencil or a sharp stick, and some yarn or string.

1. Outside, build a hill out of damp sand or soil on a wooden board.

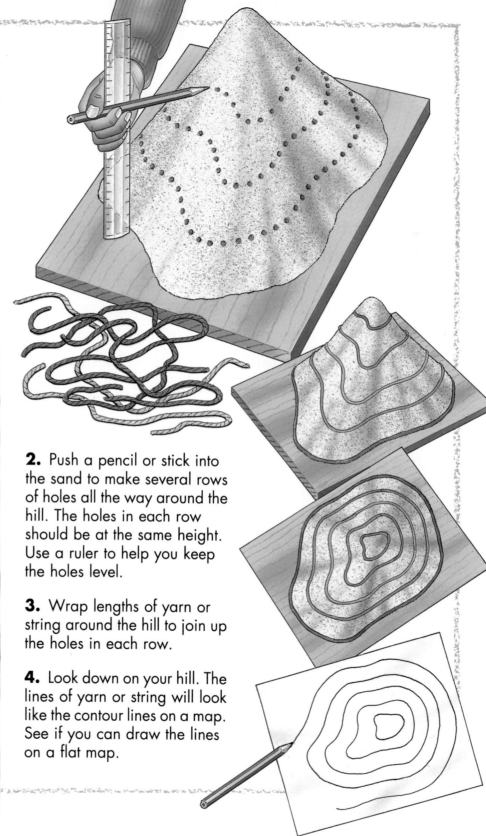

The bands or contour lines tell you that the small hill is 40 feet high and the large hill is 100 feet high. The contour lines also show you that one side of the small hill is steeper than the other.

2. Push a pencil or stick into the sand to make several rows of holes all the way around the hill. The holes in each row should be at the same height. Use a ruler to help you keep the holes level.

3. Wrap lengths of yarn or string around the hill to join up the holes in each row.

4. Look down on your hill. The lines of yarn or string will look like the contour lines on a map. See if you can draw the lines on a flat map.

Finding a Place

Have you ever tried to find a town or a road on a map? The easiest way is to use the map's index. This will probably give you some numbers or letters alongside the name of the place you want. These numbers and letters refer to a network of lines dividing the map into squares. The squares are called the map grid, and the numbers and letters are the grid reference. Different countries use different grids on their maps, but they usually include instructions about how to use them.

Archaeologists give each object they find a grid reference on a plan or map. This helps them to remember exactly where everything was discovered.

Finding a Building

A grid reference refers to a square on a map. It gives numbers or letters for the two lines that cross each other at the bottom lefthand corner of each square.

The reference to the lines going up and down the map (the eastings) is given first, followed by the reference to the lines going across the map (the northings). On this map, the red building is in C5 and the blue one is in I4.

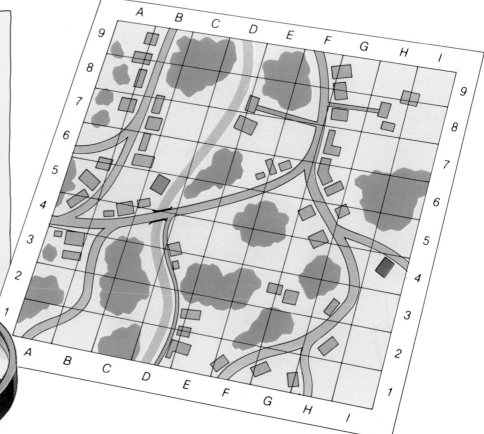

Do it yourself

See if you can give your friends a grid reference to explain exactly where you plan to meet them.

1. Use the map below or draw a rough map of your local park on some large-squared graph paper.

2. Label the grid squares across the top and bottom and up the sides. You can use letters or numbers or both, as on the map below.

3. Work out a meeting place. For example, the restaurant on the map below is in C8.

Giving Directions

Grid references make it easy to give directions without writing down a long list of instructions. If you can read a map, you should be able to find places without getting lost!

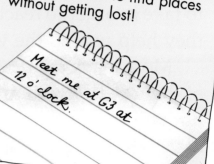

Meet me at G3 at 12 o'clock.

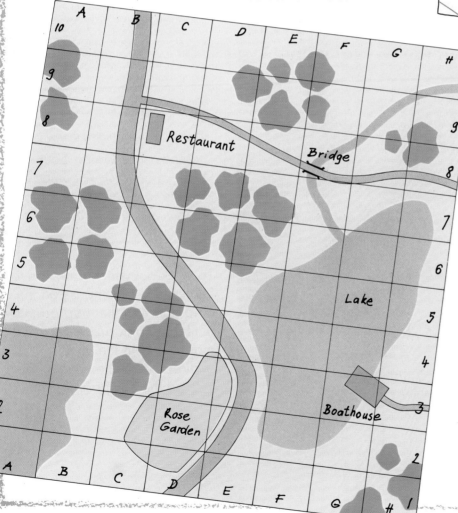

World maps also use grid lines, called lines of latitude and longitude. You can read about them on page 182.

173

Finding the Way

Maps do not only help us to find out where places are and the distances between them. They also tell us which direction to take in order to reach a place. In other words, they help us find the way.

Most maps are drawn with a North arrow at the top, as if you are facing North. To find out which direction North is really in, we use a compass. With a compass and a map, we can find our way in fog or even in a snow blizzard when it is hard to see where we are going.

Compass Directions

The four main points on a compass are North, South, East, and West. A compass needle is a tiny magnet that always points North.

To work out which direction to take, place a compass on the map and turn the map around until the North arrow on the map points in the same direction as the needle on the compass.

Do it yourself

Make your own compass with a magnetized needle, a slice of cork, and a shallow dish.

1. Ask an adult to help you magnetize the needle as shown below. You must stroke the magnet along the needle about 50 times.

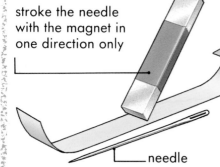

stroke the needle with the magnet in one direction only

needle

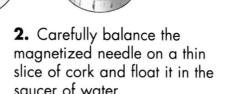

slice of cork

2. Carefully balance the magnetized needle on a thin slice of cork and float it in the saucer of water.

3. The needle will swing to North. Check this with a real compass and label North on the edge of the dish.

Where is North?

An arrow on a map pointing to "true north" is a straight and accurate line to the North Pole. But a compass needle always points to "magnetic north" because it is pulled by magnetic forces deep inside the Earth. Magnetic north is about 1,000 miles away from the true North Pole.

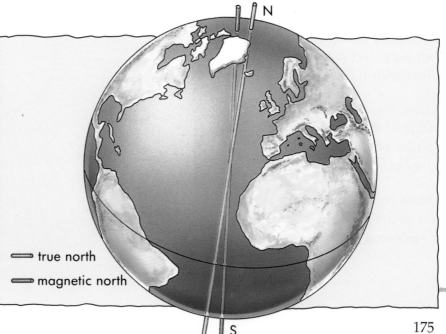

true north

magnetic north

Measuring Angles

Before they draw a map, map-makers need to know the exact position of everything to be included. To do this, the land is divided up into a network of points, and the distances and angles between the points are measured. This is called making a survey and the people who collect the information are called surveyors. To help find the angle between two points, surveyors take bearings. You can try taking a bearing using the bearing board shown below.

For hundreds of years, sailors have used sextants (which measure the angle between the Sun and the horizon) to work out their position at sea.

Do it yourself

Make a bearing board to measure an angle.

1. Ask an adult to help you make a copy of the circle shown here and extend all the lines with a ruler.

2. Label the numbers around the edge of the paper and stick the paper onto a large square board.

3. Place your bearing board on the ground. This is called your reference or base point.

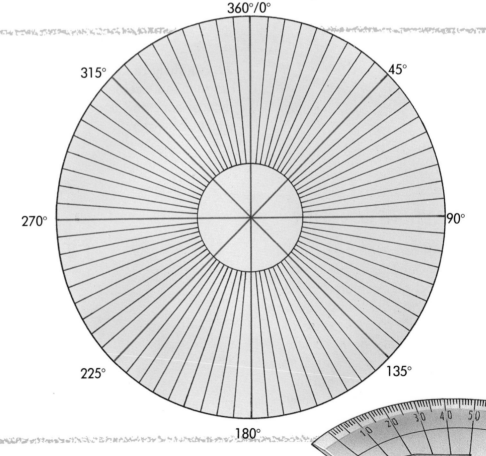

Surveyors at Work

Today, surveyors use modern electronic equipment to measure distances very accurately in just a few seconds. The instruments record how long it takes light or sound waves to travel between two points. Because we know how far light and sound travel in a certain time, it is possible to work out the distance between the two points.

4. Use a ruler to help you line up two objects you want to measure with the lines on your board. The angle between the two lines is the bearing.

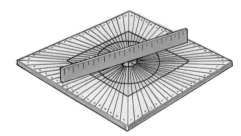

5. Read off the angle in a clockwise direction. (On this board, each space represents five degrees.)

177

Making Maps

As well as taking detailed measurements, surveyors record other information that appears on maps. This may include the type of land, such as whether it is dry or marshy, wooded or bare. Surveyors may also record the location of public buildings, like churches and schools.

Measurements taken by surveyors on the ground are backed up by photographs taken from aircraft or satellites. These photographs are called aerial photographs. They are very useful when the land is too hilly or marshy to make a ground survey.

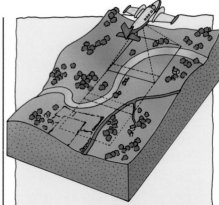

Maps from the Air

As the aircraft flies over-head, a camera takes two photographs of each section of land.

Left: Satellite photographs, like this one of San Francisco Bay, are used to make weather maps.

Below: Although maps are still drawn by hand, most map-makers now use computers.

Do it yourself

Make your own Treasure Island map!

Choose a scale for your map and draw an arrow to show the direction North. Decide how you want to show the height of the land – through colors, contour lines, or through symbols, and a key as on the map below.

You could make your map look old by crumpling up the edges and dipping the corners in tea.

Finding the Treasure

When you have finished drawing your map, add a grid and label the lines with letters and numbers.

Now decide where you are going to hide your treasure. Write some clues using grid references to guide the treasure hunters to the treasure.

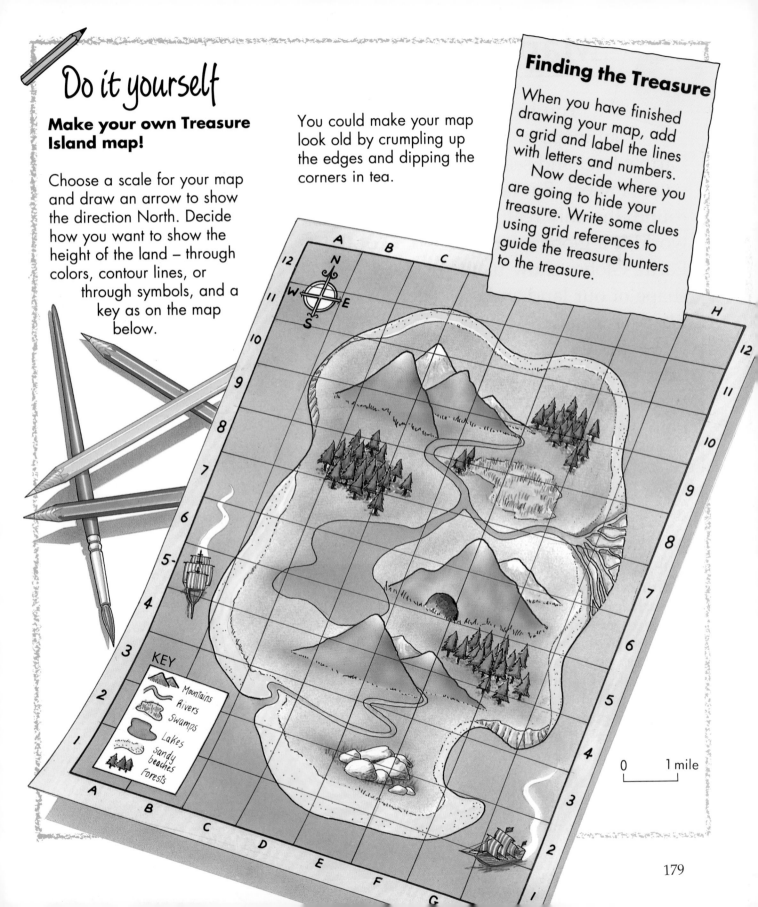

KEY

Mountains
Rivers
Swamps
Lakes
Sandy beaches
Forests

0   1 mile

Mapping the World

You have probably seen many flat maps of the world with the Earth's land and sea stretched out on one page or sheet. But because the Earth is round, the only really accurate map of the world is a globe – a round model of the Earth. Globes show us the true size and shape of our land and sea. They are also tilted at a slight angle because the Earth leans slightly to one side. But globes are hard to carry around. They cannot be folded up and put in a pocket like a flat map, so we use flat maps more often.

The only place that we can see the true size and shape of the world's land and oceans is in space, on satellite photographs like this one.

Do it yourself

It is not easy to make flat drawings of the Earth's surface. Some pieces of land have to be stretched and others have to be shrunk. Try making your own flat map from a globe. You will need tracing paper, a pencil, and tape.

Ask a friend to hold the globe steady while you trace around the shapes of the large land areas.

Old Maps

Hundreds of years ago most people believed that the Earth was flat, like a giant tabletop. They thought they would fall off the edge if they sailed far enough out to sea.

This map was drawn about 500 years ago. Although it is not accurate, it is easy to recognize the shapes of the different land areas. Can you recognize parts of Europe and Africa?

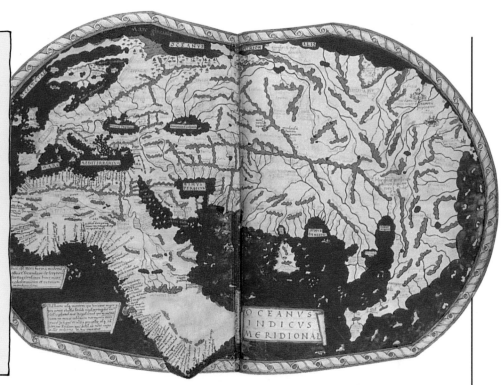

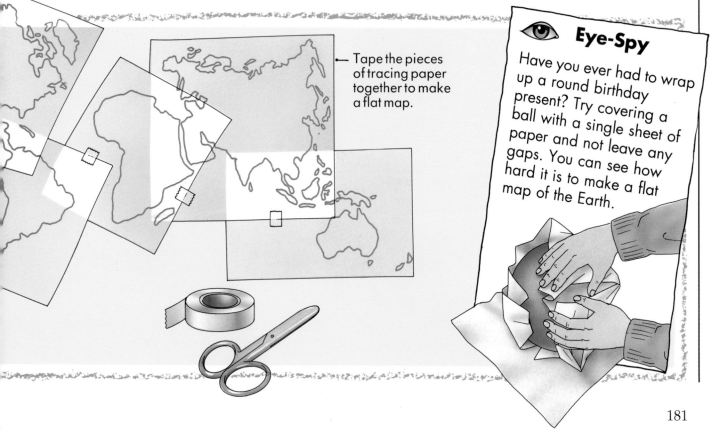

← Tape the pieces of tracing paper together to make a flat map.

Eye-Spy

Have you ever had to wrap up a round birthday present? Try covering a ball with a single sheet of paper and not leave any gaps. You can see how hard it is to make a flat map of the Earth.

Latitude and Longitude

On globes and on maps showing large areas of the world, we can find a place by using a grid of imaginary lines called lines of latitude and longitude. Lines of longitude, or meridians, run up and down the map or globe. They are measured in degrees east or west of a line drawn through Greenwich, in England. Lines of latitude, or parallels, are measured in degrees north or south of the equator – an imaginary line that circles Earth's middle.

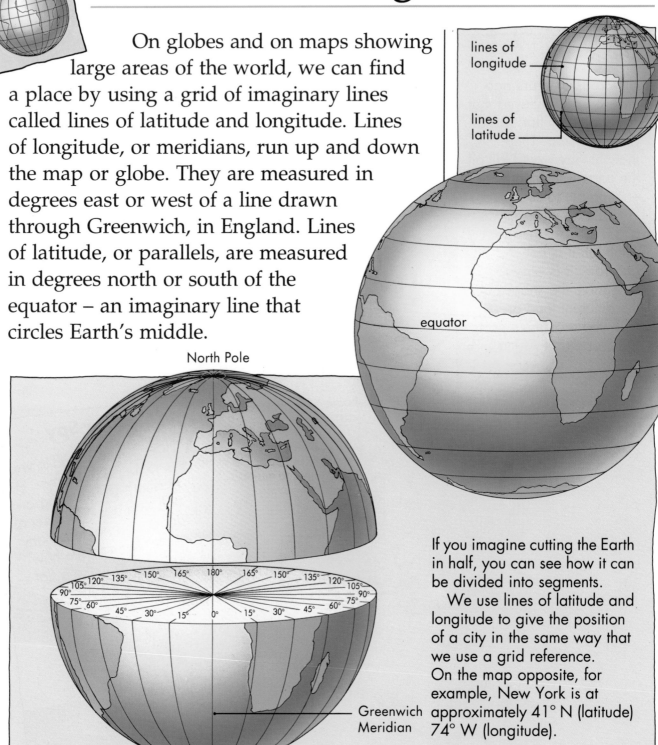

lines of longitude

lines of latitude

equator

North Pole

105° 120° 135° 150° 165° 180° 165° 150° 135° 120° 105°
90° 90°
75° 60° 75°
45° 30° 15° 0° 15° 30° 45° 60°

Greenwich Meridian

South Pole

If you imagine cutting the Earth in half, you can see how it can be divided into segments.

We use lines of latitude and longitude to give the position of a city in the same way that we use a grid reference. On the map opposite, for example, New York is at approximately 41° N (latitude) 74° W (longitude).

182

The Great Meridian

The 0° line of longitude can be seen as a line on the ground in Greenwich, England. It is sometimes called the Great or Prime Meridian.

Every place in the world that lies on this line has the same time, called Greenwich Mean Time, or GMT for short. Every 15° east or west of the Greenwich Meridian, the time changes. East, the time is behind Greenwich and west, it is ahead.

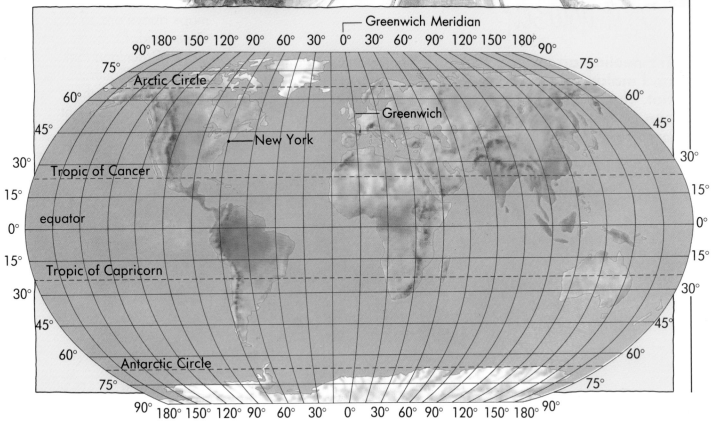

Map Projections

A projection is the way in which mapmakers show the curved surface of the Earth on a flat map. There are over 200 kinds of map projection, but they all distort or change the shape and size of our continents or the distances between them. This distortion is greatest on maps of the whole world. Mapmakers choose a particular map projection depending on what they need to show.

Three main kinds of map projection are shown at the top of the opposite page.

Eye-Spy

Look at different atlases (books of maps) to compare the size and shape of one country in various projections. The maps above are all of Greenland. On some maps, Greenland looks bigger than South America, but South America is really eight times bigger!

Do it yourself

Try peeling an orange and making the peel lie flat. There is no way you can do this without breaking the peel.

To flatten out a world map, mapmakers may divide the land into pieces, rather like the segments of an orange.

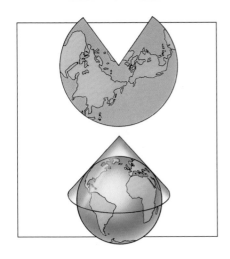

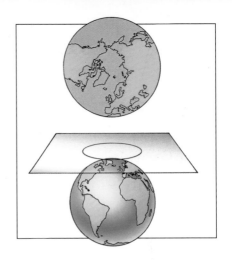

Conic Projection

This map is drawn as if a cone of paper has been placed over the globe, touching it along one line of latitude.

Cylindrical Projection

A cylindrical projection is made as it the globe has been wrapped in a tube, or a cylinder, of paper.

Azimuthal Projection

An azimuthal projection is made as if a flat sheet of paper touches the globe at one point in the center of the map.

The pieces are then arranged side by side and the "gaps" are filled in, or stretched, to make a flat map like the one on the right. This map is a cylindrical projection. The gray areas have all been stretched.

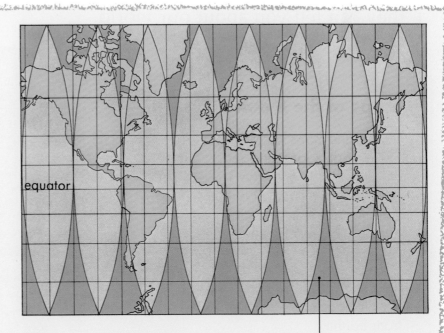

equator

stretched areas of land and sea

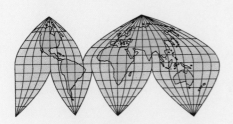

The map above is called a sinusoidal projection. Here, the globe has been cut up in

such a way that the land areas all have the correct shape and size.

Using Maps

If you look around, you will be able to see lots of different maps. Maps can show almost anything, from the number of houses in a city, or the cities in a country, to the sites of battles, the number of people in a place or the weather. Because areas change very quickly, new maps are regularly drawn with up-to-date information. See if you can find some old maps of your town in your local library. How has it changed over the years?

Now that you know more about maps, you will be able to discover how much they can tell you about our world.

Tourist Maps

Tourist maps are usually full of pictures of places to visit. They are rarely drawn to scale but they are fun and easy to use.

Maps of the Moon

Most of the maps we use are of the Earth's land and sea. But this photograph shows a map of the Moon's North Pole. It names all the craters, trenches, and valleys on the Moon's surface.

Maps like this could be used to plot the landing sites of spacecraft launched from Earth.

Mapmakers have also drawn maps of the stars in the sky, called star charts.

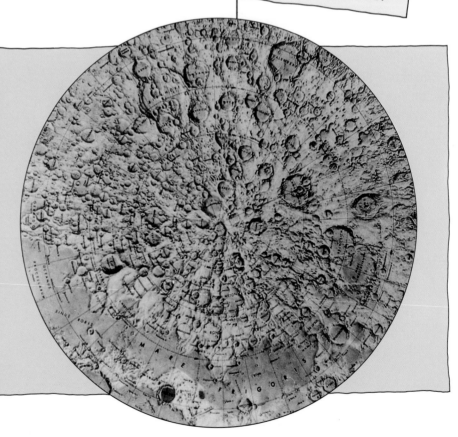

NATURE IN DANGER

Where Animals Live

Plants and animals are found almost everywhere on Earth—in the air, on the land, underground, and in the water. Each living thing belongs to a particular kind of place, called its habitat. For example, cacti grow in the desert, jellyfish are found in the sea, and parrots live in tropical forests. When people cut down trees to make way for roads and farms or pour harmful chemicals into the environment, they damage these habitats and destroy the wildlife.

There are many different types of habitat in the world, from the tropical rain forests to the polar ice caps. This picture shows the kinds of animal that live in some of these habitats.

Reefs at Risk

Coral reefs are home to many sea creatures and plants. Unfortunately, they are threatened by people who are polluting the oceans and damaging their habitat.

tropical rain forest
jaguar

grassland
gazelle

deciduous woodland
mouse

river
trout

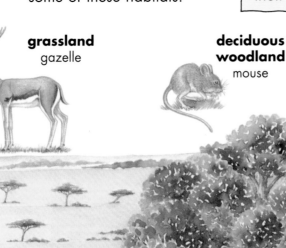

Do it yourself

Find out what type of habitat wood lice like best.

1. First, find some wood lice by looking under logs and bark.

2. Then spread a thin layer of cotton batting onto a small tray or box lid. Number the four corners of the tray with labels as shown here.

3. Cover half the tray with newspaper while you spray areas 1 and 2 with water. The batting should be damp but not soaking wet.

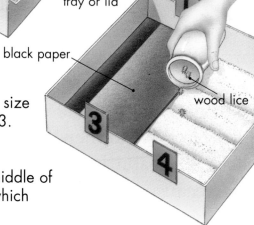

water spray

cotton batting

newspaper

tray or lid

black paper

wood lice

4. Lay a piece of black paper cut to size over areas 1 and 3.

5. Now put your wood lice in the middle of the tray and see which area they go to.

How It Works

You have divided the tray into four areas—(1) dark and damp, (2) light and damp, (3) dark and dry, and (4) light and dry. Wood lice prefer dark, damp habitats, so they will go to area 1.

mountain
eagle

coniferous forest
wolf

ocean
whale

polar regions
polar bear

👁 Eye-Spy

If you want to see some animals in their natural habitat, turn over a log in your yard or local park. How many different creatures can you find?

Keeping the Balance

Plants and animals that share the same habitat rely on each other for their survival. A delicate balance exists between them which depends largely on the amount of food available. Plants are able to make their own food, but animals have to find ready-made food. Some animals only eat plants—they are called herbivores. Other animals feed off the plant-eaters. These are the carnivores, or meat-eaters. But the balance is easily upset. For example, if fishermen catch too many sand eels, the seabirds that feed on the eels may die because they have no more food.

People upset the balance of nature when they cut down large areas of forest. The animals whose lives depend on the trees for food and shelter soon die.

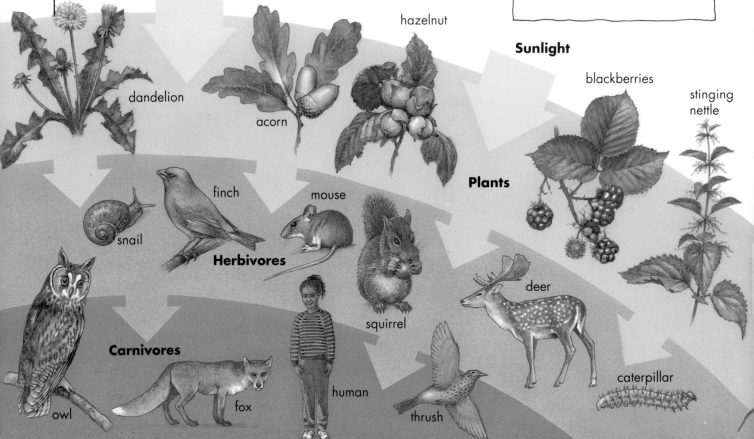

hazelnut

Sunlight

blackberries

stinging nettle

dandelion

acorn

Plants

finch

mouse

snail

Herbivores

squirrel

deer

owl

Carnivores

human

fox

thrush

caterpillar

Do it yourself

See a food chain in action.

1. Find a small leafy shoot that has a few aphids on it. (Try looking on roses or nasturtiums.) Put the shoot into a small bottle of water and plug the mouth of the bottle with tissue paper.

2. Put the bottle in a large glass jar. Cover the top with thin woven fabric—from an old handkerchief or a pair of panty hose. Use a rubber band to hold it in place.

3. Watch the aphids for a few days through a magnifying glass. Can you see them sucking juices out of the plant?

4. Now put a ladybug into the jar and watch it feed on the aphids. Which animal is the herbivore and which is the carnivore?

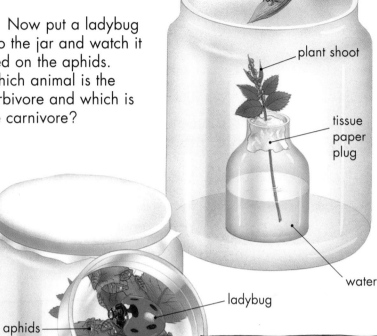

plant shoot

tissue paper plug

water

aphids

ladybug

A Woodland Food Web

This diagram on the left shows "what eats what" in a woodland habitat. Energy for life begins with the Sun. Plants use the energy from sunlight to make food. Herbivores (in the orange band) eat the plants and are then eaten by the carnivores. Try to pick out a simple food chain; for example, an acorn is eaten by a mouse which is then eaten by an owl. Can you work out any other food chains?

grass

A Delicate Balance

Kestrels are predators of mice —that is, they feed on them. When there are lots of mice, the kestrel has plenty of food and produces many young. But if the mouse population goes down, so does the number of kestrels.

Pollution Problems

One of the many threats to our wildlife is waste. In nature, waste materials such as dead plants and animals are quickly broken down and recycled. But much of the waste we produce is harmful and difficult to get rid of. Harmful waste is called pollution. Some of the most damaging pollution is caused by factories and cars. They produce fumes that turn the rain acid. Acid rain has killed millions of trees. If we want to protect our environment, we must learn to cut down on the amount of pollution we are producing.

You can see waste almost everywhere you look—in the home, on the roads, in cities, and on farms. Garbage is buried in the countryside, liquid waste is poured into rivers and oceans, and harmful fumes are pumped into the air.

acid rain

factory fumes

farming chemicals

garbage

liquid waste from factories

transportation fumes

Litter That Kills

Litter can be dangerous to wildlife. Sometimes small animals, such as mice and voles, climb into bottles, only to find they cannot get out again. Without food, they soon starve to death.

How Can We Help?

- Don't drop litter. It may be a death trap.
- Cut down on pollution by using the car less. Ride a bicycle or walk on short trips.
- If you spot bad pollution, write a letter of complaint to your local government.

Algal Blooms

Sometimes you may find a thick green blanket of algae (tiny plants) floating on a river or pond. This is called an algal bloom. Eventually it leads to the death of fish living in the water. An algal bloom occurs when fertilizers from local farmland drain into a river or pond, causing the algae to grow very fast.

Do it yourself

Find out how polluted your local stream or pond is by discovering which creatures live in the water.

Sweep a dipping net through the water to catch some tiny animals. Use this chart to identify your animals and find out how polluted the water is.

Some animals can only live in unpolluted water. If you find these, you know your water is clean. Others can survive in badly polluted water.

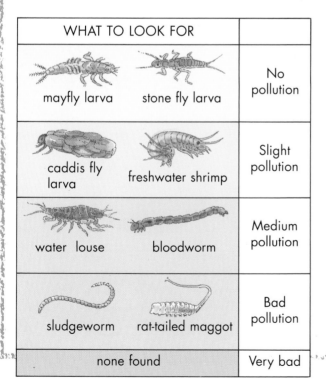

WHAT TO LOOK FOR		
mayfly larva	stone fly larva	No pollution
caddis fly larva	freshwater shrimp	Slight pollution
water louse	bloodworm	Medium pollution
sludgeworm	rat-tailed maggot	Bad pollution
none found		Very bad

Turn to page 199 to find out how to make and use a dipping net.

Wonderful Woodlands

Your local woodlands are important habitats because they are home to so many different plants and animals. The leaves and branches of the trees form a canopy high above the ground, providing shelter and food for birds and mammals. Leaf litter covers the woodland floor. It is teeming with creatures such as spiders, beetles, thrips, centipedes, and wood lice. When woods are cut down to make way for roads, factories, farms, and expanding towns, all of these wonderful animals lose their homes.

Do it yourself

Grow a tree from seed.

1. Fill a small flowerpot or yogurt container with potting soil. Make a hole in the soil about 1.5in. deep. Push a seed into the hole and cover it with soil.

2. Put your pot in a warm sunny place and keep the soil damp. By spring, you may have a young sapling. Dig a small hole outside in a shady spot and plant your tree in it, along with its soil.

squirrel

bird's nest

moth

lichen

beetle

moss

fox

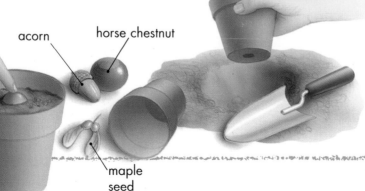

sapling

acorn

horse chestnut

maple seed

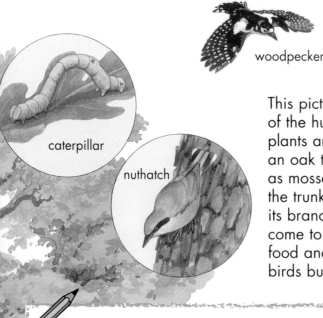

woodpecker

caterpillar

nuthatch

This picture shows just a few of the hundreds of different plants and animals that live in an oak tree. Small plants such as mosses and ferns grow on the trunk. Insects move among its branches. Small mammals come to the tree in search of food and shelter. And many birds build their nests in trees.

How Can We Help?

- Plant your own tree (see opposite page).
- Join an organization that plants trees and cares for woodlands.
- If your local woods are under threat, start a petition with family and friends asking your town to save it.

Do it yourself

Do a tree survey to find out as much as you can about a tree near you. Keep all your results in a special book.

1. Take a photograph of your tree in each season. Stand in the same spot each time to get the same view.

2. Collect a winter twig, a spring bud, a summer flower, and a fall fruit or seed.

photographs

3. Find out how old your tree is by measuring around the trunk about 3 feet above the ground. Count one year for every 1 inch you measure.

4. Take leaf and bark rubbings using a wax crayon and paper. Press some leaves in your book as well—one for each season.

5. Use a field guide to identify what kind of plants and animals are living in and around your tree.

leaf rubbing

bark rubbing

Forests in Danger

Trees are very useful plants. As well as being home to a wealth of wildlife, their wood can be used for making paper, for building homes and furniture, and as fuel. Also, when plants make food from sunlight, they use up a gas called carbon dioxide and release the gas oxygen. People breathe in oxygen and breathe out carbon dioxide, and trees help to balance the level of these gases in the air. Yet all around the world, forests are rapidly being destroyed for timber or to grow crops.

More than half the world's rain forests have already been destroyed. If we continue to cut them down, there will be no forests left 50 years from now.

👁 Eye-Spy

Go into each room at home and see how many things you can find that come from trees. Here are some ideas.

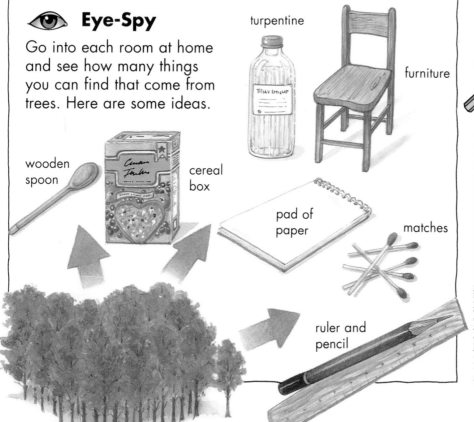

turpentine

furniture

wooden spoon

cereal box

pad of paper

matches

ruler and pencil

Do it yourself

Show that plants give off a gas.

1. Fill a bowl or glass tank with water. Put a glass or jar into the water and tip it up so that all the air escapes.

2. Place some pondweed in the glass without letting any air back in. (You can buy pondweed from a pet shop.)

Drugs from the Forest

Did you know that many of our medicines are made from plants that grow in the rain forest? Drugs made from this rosy periwinkle are used to treat leukemia. Unless we save the remaining rain forests, we will lose many useful plants that could save lives.

rosy periwinkle

Rain forests are home to at least three-fourths of all the world's wildlife. Millions of different kinds of plant and animal live there, but many of them have not yet been discovered.

How Can We Help?

- Don't waste paper—you are also wasting trees.
- Collect newspapers and cardboard for recycling.
- When people buy new furniture, they should check that it is not made of wood from the rain forests, such as teak and mahogany.

3. Turn the glass upside down in the water and sit it on three small blobs of modeling clay. Make sure you leave a small gap underneath the glass.

4. Leave the tank for a few days in a warm sunny place. Watch the gas bubbling off the plant and collecting at the top of the glass. This gas is oxygen, produced by the plant as it makes food.

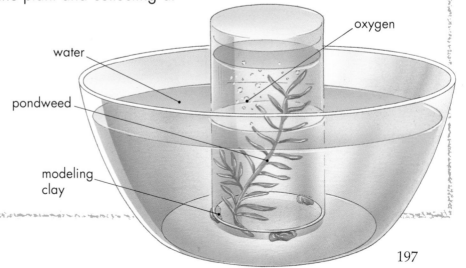

water

oxygen

pondweed

modeling clay

Rivers, Ponds, and Lakes

Clean, fresh water is home to a wide variety of wildlife. Animals such as fish, snails, crayfish, and insects live in the water itself, dragonflies and mayflies skim across the surface, water birds live close by, and water plants flourish on the banks. But many of our rivers, ponds, and lakes have become polluted by waste chemicals that pour into them from farms and factories. Sometimes only the hardiest plants and animals survive in the filthy water.

A healthy river is teeming with wildlife living in and around the water. A polluted stretch of river has little life in it. The dirty water often smells and may be full of all kinds of litter. An algal bloom may float on the water's surface.

Fisherman's Threat

Waterbirds sometimes get tangled in fishing lines left on riverbanks by careless fishermen. The birds may die if the line gets too tight around their throats.

algal bloom

litter

heron

iris

kingfisher

dragonfly

diving beetle

trout

crayfish

stickleback

water snail

minnows

Clean-Up Campaign

Many young people spend some of their spare time helping to clean up their local river or pond, making it much safer for wildlife. Find out if there is a clean-up campaign near you that you can join.

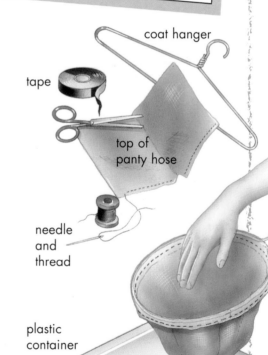

Do it yourself

Make your own pond dipping net.

1. Ask an adult to cut a piece off a metal coat hanger about 28in. long. Bend the wire into a circle leaving 2in. at each end, then poke the ends into a bamboo stick. Tape the ring in place with duct tape.

2. Cut the legs off a pair of panty hose. Sew the cut edges together to make a "bag" out of the waist part.

3. Fold the top edge of the panty hose over the wire and sew it down to hold the bag firmly in place. You are now ready to use your net.

4. Take a large plastic container with you to keep your animals in, plus a magnifying glass. When you have caught some animals in your net, do not pick them up with your fingers—you may squash them. Instead, turn the net inside out and lower it into the water inside the container. Always put the animals back when you have finished looking at them.

coat hanger

tape

top of panty hose

needle and thread

plastic container

dipping net

magnifying glass

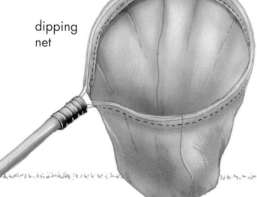

Save Our Seas

Today, our seas are under threat. We rely on the seas to provide us with food, particularly fish. But we are catching far too many fish, so their numbers are going down rapidly. Pollution, too, is a problem. For many years, people thought that getting rid of waste at sea was safe and that it would be quickly diluted. But poisons build up in the water and affect the health of sea animals. All over the world, dolphins and seals are dying from new diseases and fish are found with strange-looking growths on their skin.

Almost three-fourths of the Earth's surface is covered by water. Yet we manage to pollute much of it and make fish stocks dangerously low.

Animals such as dolphins, turtles, and sharks often get caught up in fishing nets. Purse seine nets are like huge bags, whereas drift nets are more like curtains. Both of these nets can be death traps. Long lines are much better because they only catch the fish that are wanted.

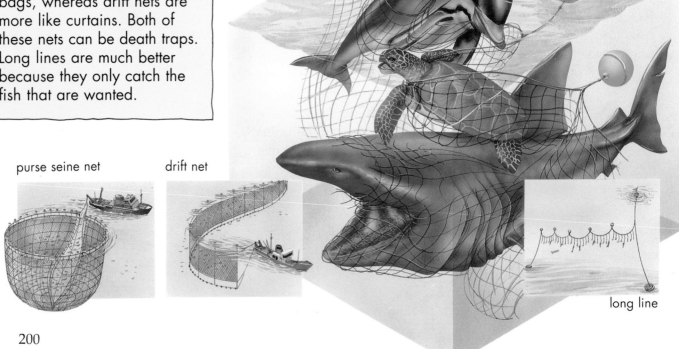

purse seine net

drift net

long line

200

Do it yourself

Do this simple test to see how oil damages a bird's feathers.

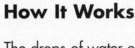

clean feather

oily feather

1. Collect two feathers. Then rub a few drops of bicycle oil or lubricating oil onto one of the feathers using some cotton balls.

2. Pour a few drops of water on to each feather and see what happens.

How It Works

The drops of water on the clean feather roll off because the feather is waterproof. Too much oil destroys the waterproofing, so the water soaks into the oily feather and spoils its shape. Birds with oily feathers cannot fly or dive and soon die from cold and hunger.

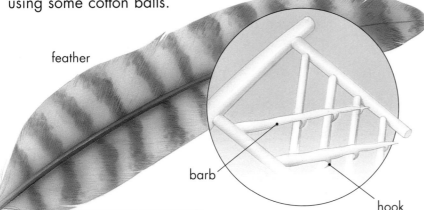

feather

barb

hook

More Things To Try

The barbs of a feather are attached to one another with hooks, rather like Velcro. Oil damages the feathers so that the hooks no longer work and the bird cannot fly.

With a magnifying glass look at the hooks on a feather. Try breaking the hooks apart then joining them up again like a zipper. This effect means that even if the feathers break apart in stormy weather, the bird can always "zip" them up again by preening them into shape.

Oil tankers move millions of tons of oil around the world each year. When there is an accident, oil spills into the sea, where it causes terrible damage to wildlife. Thousands of seabirds may die. If the birds are rescued quickly, the oil can be removed from their feathers by washing them carefully in detergents such as dishwashing liquid.

Farming Takes Over

The number of people in the world has increased rapidly over the last two hundred years, and it is still increasing. All these extra mouths need food to eat, and farming has had to keep up with the demand. Natural habitats are destroyed to make way for huge fields. Chemicals are sprayed onto the fields to increase the yield (output). There are fertilizers to feed the crops and pesticides to kill pests. But these chemicals cause pollution, and pesticides kill more than just the pests.

Free-Range

Many farm animals live indoors, packed together with no room to move. But some farmers let their animals roam free outdoors. These animals are called free-range.

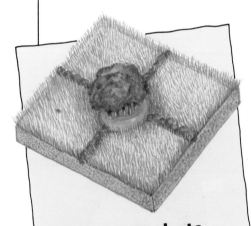

Natural Pockets

To avoid using harmful pesticides, some farmers grow small pockets of woodland in the corners of their fields. Many of the animals that live there feed on the pests.

On a farm, the huge fields are usually planted with a single crop and sprayed with chemicals. Few plants and animals are found living here.

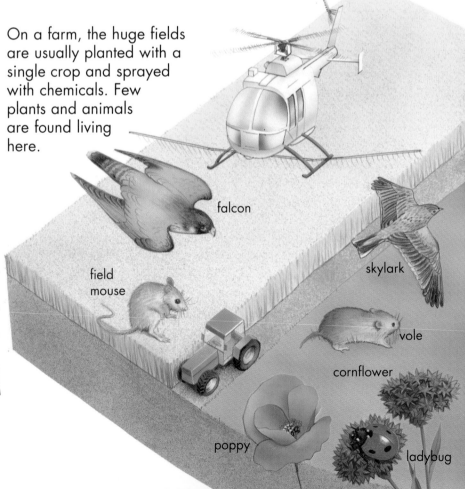

falcon

field mouse

skylark

vole

cornflower

poppy

ladybug

Combine harvesters are used to cut down crops. But they also destroy small animals that get in their way.

In comparison to farmland, natural meadows and woodlands are rich in wildlife. It is important to protect these habitats.

falcon

frog

bit

butterfly

primrose

daisy

Do it yourself

Worms are farmers' friends. As they burrow through the soil, they mix it all up and let air into it. This helps to keep the soil healthy. You can watch worms at work by making a worm farm.

1. Take a large glass jar and fill it with three layers of different soils—gravel or sand, mud from a stream, and ordinary soil will do.

2. Add a layer of leaves. Then put four or five worms on top.

3. Wrap black paper around your worm farm to keep it dark and make sure the soil is kept moist. Check it after a day or two to see what has happened.

City Living

Modern cities are really jungles of concrete and asphalt. Yet a city habitat is very different from a natural habitat such as woods. Despite this, wildlife can be found even in the center of the world's busiest cities. Animals are attracted to cities because there is a vast and never-ending supply of free food, such as the food that gets thrown out with our garbage. Many birds and mammals make their homes in parks and tree-lined roads, whereas animals such as rats and mice live beneath the cities in the sewers and drains.

👁 **Eye-Spy**

You have to look quite carefully to spot some city dwellers. Old walls may be home to a host of tiny plants and animals. How many creatures can you find living on a wall?

Cities can be home to some unlikely guests including moose, monkeys, raccoons, and foxes. Others animals, such as rats and mice, are more common inhabitants.

moose in Canadian and Scandinavian towns

rats

fox

pigeons

vervet monkeys in towns in Africa

mice

storks often nest on rooftops in northern European towns

Polar bears are among the largest visitors to towns—and the most dangerous! Many are attracted by the free supply of food to be found in garbage dumps.

Do it yourself

Attract birds to your backyard or school ground by putting out bird food.

To make a coconut cake, melt 8oz. of lard or suet. Mix in 1lb of raisins, peanuts, bread and cake crumbs, sunflower seeds, and oatmeal. Put the mix into half a coconut shell and let it set before you hang it up outside.

Make a string of peanuts in the shell by threading the nuts together using a large needle and strong thread.

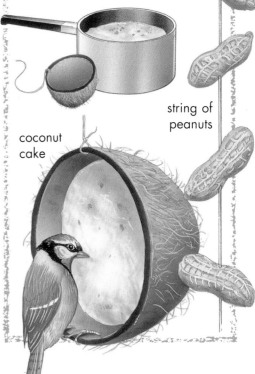

string of peanuts

coconut cake

raccoons are found in cities in the U.S.A.

Hunting and Collecting

People have hunted animals for food and skins for thousands of years. Today, animals are hunted for sport or for their horns, tusks, bones, or fur. Hunting and collecting threatens the survival of many creatures. There are now laws to protect some animals, such as the law banning the trade in elephant ivory. Sadly, animals such as big cats are still hunted, even though they are protected by law. The poachers can make lots of money by selling their fur.

 Eye-Spy

When you are on vacation, look out for souvenirs and objects in the stores that are made from wild animals, such as ivory ornaments, crocodile skin bags, coral, sponges, and shells. Would you want to buy any of these?

Elephant tusks are made of ivory, which is very valuable. Poachers have killed thousands of elephants in Africa, but trade in ivory is now banned and the poaching has almost stopped.

Do it yourself

Hunting animals may be cruel but tracking them is not, and it can be great fun.

Next time you go for a walk, look for any tracks or signs left by animals. See if you can figure out what kind of animals they were. Things to look for include bits of fur, feathers, footprints, leftover food, animal footpaths in the grass, and droppings.

How Can We Help?

- Don't collect birds' eggs, butterflies, wild-flowers, or any other living thing.
- If you collect wild animals such as snails or pond creatures to study, keep them only for a short time and always return them to their natural habitat afterward.
- Don't kill animals just because you don't like them—spiders, moths, ants, and slugs are just as important as bigger animals.

Big cats such as leopards and tigers have been killed for their beautiful fur. Many people believe fur looks better worn by the cat—not when worn by a person.

rat prints

hazelnut eaten by a squirrel

hazelnut eaten by a mouse

pine cone eaten by a squirrel

fur caught on barbed wire

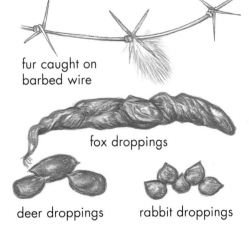

fox droppings

deer droppings

rabbit droppings

squirrel prints (back paws)

mouse prints

deer prints

Small mammals have their own particular way of eating nuts and pine cones, so look out for these signs.

You can usually recognize animal droppings by their shape. Also look for fur caught on barbed wire.

Each animal has its own set of footprints. They often show up best in mud or snow. See if you can find any of these footprints.

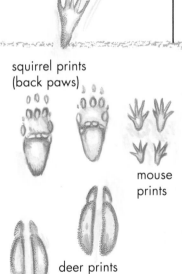

fox prints

207

Endangered Wildlife

Many plants and animals have disappeared completely from Earth. That is, they have become extinct. Sometimes this happens naturally. Dinosaurs may have died out because of a sudden change in climate. But many species are now extinct because of humans. Destruction of habitat is the biggest threat to wildlife. It has made animals, such as the giant panda, become endangered—that is there are only a few thousand individuals, or even fewer, left in the world.

Special organizations such as Greenpeace try to protect endangered animals. Here, they are trying to stop whaling.

Extinct!

The dodo was a large flightless bird that lived in Mauritius. An easy catch for sailors, the last one was killed in 1700.

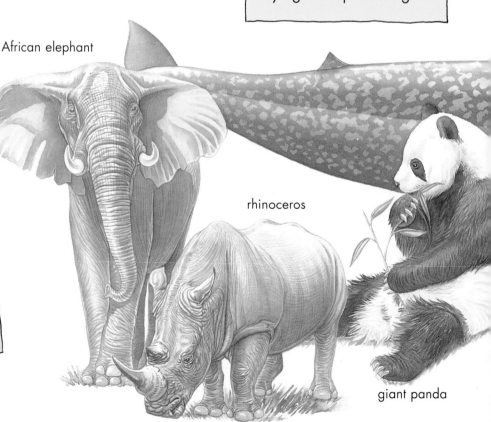

African elephant

rhinoceros

giant panda

Running Wild

Wolves were once a common sight in the United States and Europe. But they caught sheep and cattle, so they were shot by farmers. They are now being reintroduced to places where they once roamed wild.

Countryside Code

Many of us can do little to help tigers and whales, but we can all help to conserve wildlife by following a few simple rules when we go into nature reserves and parks.

Many well-known animals are endangered. If these animals are not protected, and their habitats conserved, they may soon disappear forever. Imagine what the world would be like without tigers, elephants, pandas, and whales!

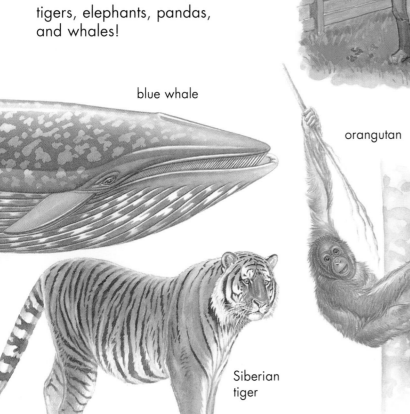

blue whale

orangutan

Siberian tiger

- Do not pick any wild-flowers, even if there are plenty of them.
- Keep to the paths so you do not trample wildflowers.
- Keep your dog on a leash if there are animals or nesting birds around.
- Close gates so that farm animals do not escape.

Make a Nature Reserve

It is easy to attract wildlife into our yards, especially birds. Climbing plants and bushes give the birds shelter, an upturned garbage can lid makes a good birdbath, and plants such as teasels and globe thistles provide food. Grow grass long if you want to attract insects—even a pile of logs and flowerpots can be home to a surprising number of animals.

Attracting Butterflies

- Buddleia, poppies, sedum, scabious, and lavender are all good for attracting butterflies, which feed off their sweet nectar.
- Ragwort and cabbages are good food plants for caterpillars.

Turn a corner of your yard into a nature reserve. Build a pond to attract a wealth of wildlife, from snails and dragonflies to frogs, newts, and maybe the occasional duck. Piles of logs will house insects, centipedes, spiders, and toads. And a compost heap for kitchen waste and grass cuttings will become home to worms and toads.

Index

Acknowledgments

Photographs: [**Energy and Power**] Ecoscene pp. 11, 13 (Morgan), 22 (Glover), 24 (Cooper), 26 (Winkley), 27 (Jones); Robert Harding Picture Library p. 14; NHPA p. 32 (E. Soder); Panos Pictures p. 16 (R. Giling); Science Photo Library pp. 8 (G. Garradd), 12 (D. Lovegrove), 19 (U.S. Dept. of Energy), 21 (H. Morgan), 25 (M. Bond); ZEFA pp. 9, 29 (J. Blanco); [**Batteries, Bulbs, and Wires**] Taheshi Takahara/Science Photo Library p. 52; ZEFA pp. 35, 44, 50, 58; [**Sound and Light**] Hutchinson Library p. 73; Kanehara Shuppan Co., Ltd. p. 83; Life File Photo Library p. 78; NHPA pp. 71, 83, 84; ZEFA pp. 61, 66, 68; [**Solids and Liquids**] David Glover p.96; J. Allan Cash Ltd. p. 102; Robert Harding Picture Library p. 103; Hutchinson Library p. 106; ZEFA pp. 92, 98, 105; [**Weather and Climate**] Hutchinson Library p. 113; NASA p. 109; NOAA p. 127; Orion Press/ZEFA p. 120; ZEFA pp. 125, 126, 129, 130; [**Rivers and Oceans**] Harold Berger p. 138; Alan Cork p. 147; Dennis Gilbert p. 156; Hutchinson Library pp. 143, 144, 148; ZEFA p. 141; [**Maps and Mapping**] British Library p. 181; Earth Satellite Corporation/Science Photo Library p. 178; Marconi Underwater Systems p. 169; NASA pp. 180, 186; Christine Osbourne Pictures p. 177; [**Nature in Danger**] Ecoscene pp. 190 (W. Lawler), 193 (N. Hawkes), 196 (E. Schaffer), 203 (N. Hawkes); NHPA pp. 198 (B. Jones and M. Shimlock), 199 (D. Woodfall), 201 (R. Tidman), 207 (M. Wendler), 209; Oxford Scientific Films (L. Lee Rue) p. 205.